Arouna
Meerbrook

Compiled by Sheila Hine

CHURNET VALLEY BOOKS
1 King Street, Leek, Staffordshire. ST13 5NW 01538 399033
thebookshopleek.co.uk
© Sheila Hine and Churnet Valley Books 2004
Most of the photographs and illustrations in this book
are the personal property of local people and are copyright

ISBN 1 904546 23 4

Printed and bound by Bath Press

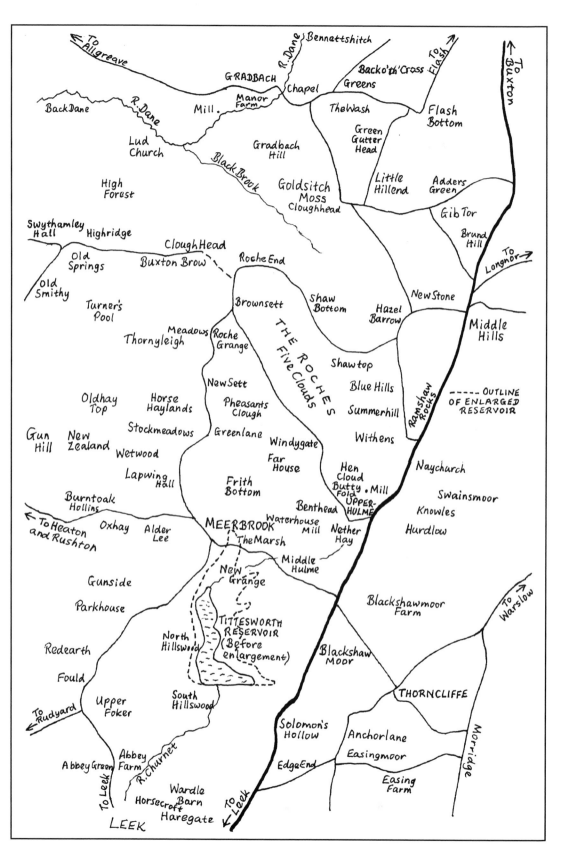

AROUND MEERBOOK
Drawn by Ray Poole

CONTENTS

4

Three Horshoes, Meerbrook.
Bill Allen and Jack Barlow.

Above: Mr Allen Snr,
Horse Haylands Farm,
taking his milk.

Bernard Allen's milk
lorry early 1960s.

Hilda Allen

Dad was born in 1904. He left school when he was twelve and went to work on the Okeover estate. Later he was a platelayer on the railways, and lodged with Mrs Truman at Rushton. Then he would get married and rent a small farm at Gratton, where I was born. Mum was from Leek. After a while we moved to Ford, renting another farm just over the bridge. We lived in half the farmhouse, and the owner had the other half.

While living there, Dad lost a pig farrowing, and all twelve piglets. Then forty cock chickens, when the fox got in one night; and then some cows died with Johnes disease. All in six months and he went bankrupt.

So we had to move to Buxton and start again. Mum kept a fish and chip shop on the main street as you went down into Buxton; and Dad worked in a quarry, maybe Hillhead. Then they moved up to Foxholes on Butterton Moor, then to Waterfall. I went to Onecote and Butterton schools.

In February 1943 we moved to North Hillswood Farm at Meerbrook. All the stock except calves were walked from Waterfall. We rented the farm from Mr Argles of Haregate Hall. He owned all around South Hillswood.

When Potteries Water Board decided to extend the reservoir, there was a compulsory purchase order and Mr Argles had to sell quite a bit of property. North Hillswood was about 155 acres, and about half went to the Water Board, so he decided to sell the rest to Dad.

All I can remember at North Hillswood is a lot of hard work. I wanted to be a dressmaker, but Dad said there was plenty of work without going out for it. I did anything, milking, muckspreading by hand, thistle spudding, turnip thinning.

I hated hand milking, I couldn't milk very well, and we milked a fair lot, there could have been forty. We bought cows off Fred Robinson mostly and he was always alright with us. Anything wrong and he'd take it back. I heard tell of him going to Middle Hulme to buy a calf, and when the farmer asked his price, Fred threw his arms up in the air and shouted "Whisky! Whisky!" then fell over backwards and rolled down the field.

We also kept hens, pigs and working horses. Usually a couple of lads lived in too. We all used to get some cossings, my Dad was a hard task master. When I was seventeen, Mum left Dad and went to live in Macclesfield. They got divorced - that was a major event and upheaval in those days. It would make the News of the World.

My future husband Ron, was born at Horse Haylands, and with two of his brothers, they formed a band, the other two played accordians and Ron played drums. They played at church dances, and dances for the troops. They used to take the stuff down to the village hall on a hand cart.

The first lot of Americans that came were National Guard; they were a nice lot. They used to come down to Ron's Uncle Bill's at the Three Horse Shoes, and afterwards they wrote to him for a while. They were shipped abroad and most were lost, very few lived.

I remember the Americans coming down to dances. The village hall would be half full with women, then at 10.00, when the pub closed, the men would come up and the room would be full by 10.30. We cycled to dances at Meerbrook and Rudyard, later Ron had a motorbike.

When Ron left school, he went timber felling for Evans and Bellhouse. They were

working in the woods near Hanging Stone, cutting timber for pit props and all sorts. It was a reserved job in the war. Another job was timbering up near Clitheroe. Working with crosscut saws, hand saws and axes. He's still got a hole in his leg, where he hit himself with an axe.

He also had a timbering job at Capesthorne, where he lodged with Mrs Worth. After that he drove milk wagons for Ben Wilde and Sam Holland. They'd pick churns of milk up in the area; twenty-six pick-ups on Ron's wagon at one time. They'd take the churns into Manchester, maybe dropping off at three dairies, Dobsons, Co-op or Hygenic Dairy. Then they'd go to maybe three corn mills and pick up sacks of corn which they carried on top of the load of empty churns. So then they would deliver the corn to the farms. It could be any time when they finished some nights, then an early start again next morning picking up churns.

For a while he worked at Hillswood, farming, then building for Jack Findlow, then back on lorries for George Oliver at Rushton, hauling shavings.

In 1957 we were married, and lived in part of the house at Stockmeadows for nine years, before moving to Blackshaw Lane. Those nine years were the happiest of my life. We bought our own wagon and built up our own wood shavings business. First we had to

The Three Horseshoes bar in the village, with landlord and landlady Walter and Ada Hough.

find people to fetch the shavings from. The first lot were from Smiths at Longton; later we'd fetch from Sheffield, Chesterfield and Doncaster. Doncaster was a good place, they never charged for them, they were just pleased for them to be shifted. We'd fetch from there every day if there was a load. Other places you had to pay.

When we started it was all in bags, and often you had to fill your sacks yourselves before you could load. We always took some into Wood Treatment at Bosley. They wanted as much white shavings as they could get for making into wood flour. And we'd supply broiler farms and deep litter units, as well as ordinary farms. Tom White at Yeaveley was one of our first customers for his cows.

When we took bags they all had to be tipped by hand, or if the farmer was going to tip them he had to supply us back with sacks. If we were short you got some off the bagman who went round buying sacks off farmers.

When we had the box wagon and carried them loose, the wagon had to be shovelled off by hand every time. Six or seven tons if it was sawdust, five tons if it was shavings. That's a lot of shovelling. It might not be heavy but it's very bulky. We kept the shavings business up until we retired.

Tom, David and Peter Hine at Stockmeadows.

Milk collection in churns July 1979.

Jack Bradbury at Horse Haylands
loading his milk for the final collection
in churns, 31st July 1979.

Geoff Buxton

I was born in 1933 at Rudyard. We lived at Grandad's farm, Rudyard Green, with Granddad Buxton, Granny, Arthur Coates the lad, Mum, Dad, three of us youngsters, uncle Arthur, aunty Hetty and their three children. Twelve or thirteen of us ate round one table.

So Grandad decided that my father could have these barns at Highgate and fifty-two acres and build a new house. That was in 1936 and we moved in 1937 when I was four. It cost £700 to build.

I went to five schools, starting at West Street. Then they shifted us off to Ball Haye Green, then St. Pauls, then to Horton, finishing at Mountside.

We travelled in by Byrne's bus, picked up from the gate, then round by Rudyard. There were three children at Red Earth, four from Highgate Cottage, three of us, three cousins, Bakers and Nixons, another seven; twenty of us just about here. Yet old Harry Byrne, unless it was raining, would drop us off at Pool End at night and make us walk home. When our neighbour, Bernard, was twelve, and I was five, he'd carry me on his back.

We had to go to bed early to be up early, because the buses had to take munitions workers from Leek and Cheddleton into Swynnerton, and sometimes we'd be late back; they might leave us till half past five before fetching us home. Mum would wonder where we were.

Anyway Grandad decided to expand his herd and there wasn't enough land here. We had dairy cows and accredited poultry. So he decided to take a tenancy at Roche Grange, the middle farm. This was rented off my uncle Nathan. He had owned Rudyard Hall but sold that to John Wain in 1927. So we kept the dry stock and young stock up there and made some hay, and kept the milkers at Highgate.

We'd milk about thirty-six then, fifty odd cattle altogether. So we had to walk the stock up to Roche Grange, and walk back anything that was going to calve. One person would go in front. Cyril Nixon lived with us then. We'd turn in at Crooked Chimney on High-Up, and old Mr Pimlott would be leaning over the gate. Everyone would know we were coming along and they'd all have a word, it could be a slow process.

We'd perhaps take eight or ten, sometimes a dozen. We'd make our way to Meerbrook, and get as far as the Fountain, where we'd let the cattle graze, while Dad bobbed in for a drink and sent us some crisps and chocolate out. We thought that was grand to have a rest before we carried on, past Lodge Farm where Bowers were then, past Newsett where Abraham Taylor was, up Cote Lane and we were there.

One day we were going up and we'd got old Jack Nixon with us, who worked for Grandad. We landed up there and there was nobody in, and everyone was hungry. Jack Coates lived there in the house. Well, up the side of the house there was a little window, it wouldn't be twelve inches square, they just forced it open and pushed me through into the pantry, and I went and unbolted the door and let them in. Well, in this pantry was a lovely, freshly made apple tart and a nice lump of cheese and a crusty loaf of bread. They thought it was a banquet and set into it. When Jack Coates and his wife came back they thought they'd had burglars. Well they sort of had!

We used to make hay up there and one day, 1938 or 39, there was a Jew from Salford, a poultry dealer named Sammy Saffer who came buying hens. He'd got a little two ton

Vic Rider, Jack Martin, Jack Howell and Maurice Parker.

My first van, about 1950 at Highgate.

truck and my father said "Ee, I could just do with that to fetch a load of hay, you could have my car to go round and buy your hens, and go and collect up later."

So we pulled the hen crates off, and took the truck. We put a load of hay on and set off towards home. We'd got to the bottom of Cote Lane when BANG, the back tyre blew. What a noise! Well, I was out of the cab, off to Newsett, into the house and under the table before you could batt your eye. And I wouldn't come out. Mrs Taylor eventually ticed me out with a bit of cake, she said "Frank'll take you home." Well in a bit they must have changed the wheel, pulled up outside and they were after me. They had to virtually drag me out, I thought it would explode again. That's how a child thinks isn't it?

Another time we were up there, Dad was shearing sheep in the croft behind the house. It would be the summer of 1939. Grandad was getting older and not wanting as much work, so he offered to take us children up to the barn on the Roches. When he was younger he'd worked at Roche Grange in the 1890s. So off we toiled up the hill, we thought we'd never get there, and Grandad told us the story of two horses who were kept in the barn at one time. There came a blizzard, and no one could get to them. The roof was thatched, probably with heather, and when eventually someone did get to them, they'd eaten the thatch, but they were still dead.

Up at the old barn on the Roches.

When war broke out, petrol and other fuels became tight and Dad bought a motorbike to travel up to Roche Grange with and save some fuel. Unfortunately on 15th June 1940, he collided with Fred Smith's milk wagon near Newsett, and he died from his injuries shortly afterwards. The man who was riding pillion, Wilmot Pass, only had a scratch on his head. Dad was thirty-three, a crash hat might have saved him.

So we were left, with a mortgage on the house. Mother carried on, she was used to farm work and Grandad would send some help across to do some heavy work. Time went by. My brother left school in 1944 and stayed at home. I left in 1947 and we went on from there. We managed; mother stayed till we got married and settled, then she moved to Macclesfield.

With mother being widowed, Grandad used to come across every night to see if we were all right. In wartime years it would be all blackout. One dark damp night, it would be November 1941, we'd been playing games, ludo or draughts in the front room. It was about quarter to eight, Mum said, "Come on, get washed and ready for bed." She liked us in bed soon after eight. The air raid warning went; next thing we knew; BANG, BANG, BANG, BANG. Four great explosions.

The first one was down the field, the next a hundred yards away, the third one right in the middle of a thorn hedge and from that one shrapnel came through the window of the lounge, hit the ceiling and went out of the other side window. Grandad had just shut the back door and it blew it straight off the hinges and threw him against the coalhouse door. Soot came down the chimney and the whole house shook. My brother was having a wash, and he shouted, "Wheres my moneybox?" and went under the stairs. We didn't sleep that night I'll tell you! I was all of a jibber the next night too. From one of the fields you could see barrage balloons anchored over Crewe to protect the munitions factories there and Rolls Royce. I didn't know where Crewe was till then.

We had an evacuee living with us, a ten year old girl called Marie Lamey - you said it Lemmey. A few months after war broke out, children from the cities were sent out to the countryside where it was thought they would be safer. They came on the train and our area had its allocation. They came to the pavilion at the Station Hotel, Rudyard, with their possessions in a string bag and a piece of string round their neck with a label on showing their name; and people went and picked who they wanted like choosing stock at a market.

So mother chose Marie. She had a brother who went to Bradnop. Joan Shrub went to Brassingtons at Rudyard, and stayed in the area, and Bill Badham went to Robinsons at Pheasants Clough and he stayed, married and farmed at Upperhulme before moving to East Staffordshire. Marie was a big help to mother when father was killed. She went potato picking for Grandad in the autumn and came back holding up a ten bob note, the first money she'd ever earned. When she was fourteen in 1944 she had to go back home, but she would come back for a fortnight's holiday in the summer. She kept in touch with Mum, she called her, her second mother.

At the chapel anniversary, we had a tiered stage for the Sunday school to stand on. You started off when you were little on the bottom and worked your way up as you got older. There'd be about twenty-five of us before the evacuees came, and I was about halfway up the stage. Well, about twenty of them came and filled the stage, and I was put back to the bottom. They gave us some cushions to sit on.

Sunday school was in the afternoon at two-thirty. We often walked down, then afterwards we'd dingle about as boys do. One trick was to walk across the Lake dam to the train line and put a ha'penny on the rail. When the train went over, it made a clunk and squashed it bigger; it was as good as a penny. It would be milking time before we got home.

At Horton school we used to have a watch. Someone would go outside and listen for air raid warnings. If one went off we had old sack bags which were laid around the inside of the thick outside walls and we were supposed to lie on them. They thought we'd be safer; I'd have preferred to be outside.

Another duty, there was no water but a well near Bond House, and two of you fetched water. And another duty was to fetch coal in. Mother would moan that we got black, but there was no water to wash with, only to drink. There was a garden too and we did a bit in there. I don't know how much time we spent in class with all these jobs.

As lads at home we'd hide at the back of our hayshed by the road with a stirrup pump. We could tell the sound of the American jeeps coming and as they drove past we'd squirt them with water, they were open topped, so they'd get a wetting. There'd often be four soldiers in them. And we had to cross the road with the cows, so sometimes we'd wait till we heard a jeep coming, then start the cows across so they had to wait and we could ask them for gum.

Of course there was rationing too. That went on into the 1950s. We went to Blackpool for four days in 1952 and the hotel asked us to bring ration books. In the war the sweet ration might have been two ounces a week. So we'd save that up from September to Christmas and perhaps get two pounds weight in one go. We'd stuff ourselves with chocolate and stuff till we were nearly sick.

We were glad of anything. You were allowed to kill a pig; and then there was the black market. Sylvia's uncle, from near Derby, killed a lot of lambs, and he'd supply the police, to keep in with them, and they'd warn him when the Ministry were coming, so he could hide the meat. There were all sorts of tricks. Once he put the meat in a loose box, covered it in deep straw and ran some small calves on top. When the Ministry men looked over the door, he thought it was very funny because they were looking at the meat but couldn't see it.

He had a weeping willow tree which he killed under and hung the carcases in. He dug a hole in the field with zinc sheets over to throw the waste into until he could dispose of it safely. But eventually the Ministry cottoned on and dropped on him. He grew kale around the house and was throwing the meat out of the windows to try and hide it in there, and one lot of meat is supposed to have landed at the feet of a photographer who promptly recorded it. He was taken to court and fined a thousand pounds, which was a vast amount then. But he reckoned by the time he went to court he'd made the money up, and he probably carried on quietly doing the same afterwards.

Another dodge, there was a man from Rownall near Wetley Rocks, who liked a drink at the Powys Arms. Well you couldn't take your car out without you were on business or going to market. He had a Vauxhall which he'd taken the back seat out of, and he'd put a calf in the back and go off to the pub for a drink. If he was stopped he was selling a calf. He did this regular and he'd only got to open the car door and the calf would jump in, it got quite big. It was regular then that people travelled stock in the back of their cars, maybe with their heads sticking out of the windows.

I met my wife, Sylvia at Meerbrook chapel, and I had a van that I'd go up to Alderlea in. Vinnie Clulow, who lived opposite at Broadlea, would come to the door shaking her table cloth to check what time I was going. They knew well enough though because they'd a little nine inch square television, and when my van went past the suppressors would fizz the picture. But then of course the TV programmes had finished by the time I crept off home.

We went to the dances at the "bug hut." It was called The Primrose League room in our wedding album - we had our reception there. It was a lot smaller than now. You sat on forms round the edges, and when you did the 'lancers' and everyone's feet swung round, you had to get out of the way. I remember the Allen's band, and Jack Howell's band - that was: Vic RIder, Maurice Parker and Jack Howell. When some members dropped out, the two bands joined together. They played accordions.

We did pantomimes at Rudyard; there'd perhaps come four hundred people to them. I was a giant once and David Leese had brought a hen in a cage. Joan Snape was the giants wife. I had to say, "Bring me the hen which lays the golden eggs." And she put the cage in front of me, but I couldn't see out of the mask, so I'm feeling for this hen. But when she'd put the cage down, the door had come open and the hen had walked out. So I'm saying, "O hen, lay me a golden egg." And Joan's whispering, "Th' hens gone." So I bent down so I could see, and slid me hand slowly across to grab the hen's legs. Well you know what a hen does then, they squawk and flap about. The audience loved it, they thought it was all part of the act.

Mum used to buy cows off Joe Cantrell. He'd buy in Northhampton market on a Saturday, and they'd come on the train to Rushton station on the Sunday morning, when Joe and his daughters would walk them back to Packsaddle. On Tuesday he'd get a cattle wagon from Cooper Brothers at North Rode. A big red-faced man, Johnny Wardle, drove it. All day Tuesday they'd be taking cows out to farms where Joe would maybe do a barter deal, sell a cow or two and take one back in part exchange. Then on Wednesday he'd send a load of cast cows into Leek. The cows would cost about twenty-eight pounds.

When I went TB attested in the 1950s, I sold the cows to Jack Brunt, and he carted them off. I went up to Castle Douglas, where they had a sale of two to three hundred cows every Thursday. I picked eight out, the top one cost seventy-five pounds, the cheapest, seventy-one. They were the best cows in the market. Four were Argyll Ayrshires, with black coats like silk. We liked Ayrshires - I went back and bought another six later. Then I'd go to Tom Bell's sales at Crewe to get up to about twenty. In the 1960s I'd get up to thirty. Tom Bell came down from Scotland, bringing Ayrshire cattle on the train. There'd be a sale of three hundred in July, and another three hundred in October, with monthly sales in between of about one hundred. All from Lanarkshire, all a picture. If you bid a good price, he had a bottle of whisky, and he'd say, "Give that man a glass of whisky!"

On a bank holiday or other celebration in Meerbrook, at one time they'd have a football match between the married men and the single men. Well I think it was Easter Monday 1953, we had a match in the field behind the village hall. John Hyde had just come to Meerbrook as schoolmaster, and he was playing for the married men. Well he came running down the wing, and I thought "I can tackle a scrawny school teacher." He ran straight into me, I thought I'd been hit by a train! I went backwards quick, he kept going. I learnt after that he'd been a top class rugby player, he was used to being tackled. That was a lesson -and the single men lost as usual.

Ernie Belfield took the Three Horseshoes pub in Meerbrook in March 1959, and I helped him to flit in. Local farmers would go there on a Wednesday night to pay John Cook's corn bills. Tom Sumner would go for him and take orders, and the farmers would pay him and have a bit of social. Well this night, Ernie wanted to get his bed in, and I'll always remember old Bill Allen's old iron bed was still in the bedroom, with his nightcap on it. We couldn't get it to pieces, we had to saw it up and pass it out.

Going back to Grandad Buxton, he was born at Parnell Farm, Meerbrook in 1877. He

A football match at the back of the Chapel in 1954.
Joe Gould, Eric Cooke, Tom Robinson, Les Hine,
Geoff Buxton, John Turnock, Bernard Machin, Bill Hine and Harvey Day.

went to Meerbrook school, and Isaac Brunt went with him. They both smoked a pipe from when they were nine. I reckon they'd be clay pipes then. They'd hide the pipes in a wall, and when they came out of school they'd light up and off they'd go. Both smoked a pipe till they were ninety.

When he left school aged twelve, he went to work at Roche Grange for a few shillings a year. There was a bad tempered waggoner worked there. The farmer's wife would make Grandad a turnip dumpling for his dinner, and if he didn't eat it, he had it the next day. One day they were down the fields working by the barn near the Meadows. Grandad was wall building. The old lady sent their dinner down, and as the waggoner was busy with the horses, Grandad had first look in the basket. In one end was the turnip dumpling, and in the other a nice bit of bread and cheese. So he thought, "Right, I'll have the bread and cheese." And he ate it. Along comes the waggoner, saw what had been sent and exclaimed "Wait till I see th'old varmint, the bloody birds can have this!" And he slung it as far as he could. Luckily Grandad never got in trouble for it.

Later in life at Rudyard Green, Grandad always went to Rudyard Chapel, and always smoked his pipe as we went along in the car. He used to gas us with the smoke. This one particular Sunday night he went into chapel, knocked his pipe out, as he thought, and put it in the pocket of his new raincoat. There were strong wooden forms in the schoolroom and he put his coat over one and we went into chapel for the service. Well, part way through the service we could smell smoke, so they stopped the service and looked into the schoolroom where there were flames. The seat was on fire and Grandad's raincoat was in tatters. They got some water quick and drenched it out. It left a deep burn in the seat. When he got home, Grandad never told Grandma what had happened, that he'd nearly burnt the chapel down! He just quietly bought a new raincoat.

Mary Day

I was born at Stonewalls Farm, Dilhorne in 1932. About 1936 we moved to Gunside Farm, Meerbrook. Uncle Richard owned it, and Dad and Uncle Duncan bought it off him. Later on Dad bought Uncle Duncan's share. The stock would be walked over to Gunside.

I went to Meerbrook School. We had to walk round by the road, it would take about half an hour. The first time we went, it was first playtime by the time my older sister Betty got me there because I dawdled. Mum didn't go with us. Later on, if we went by the fields it would only take us ten minutes or so. If we wore clogs and there was snow, it would ball up underneath and make walking very awkward. Going by the road, we had to go through Franklins yard where Fernihoughs live, it was Carters then. I was a timid child, and if we

saw old Mr Carter, the Grandad, we were scared. We called him the 'Orgin Man', I suppose that would be like Bogey man. He had a big beard, and he'd open the gate for the cows and sit in the hedge bottom waiting for them.

The cutting down the old road to the village was known as the 'Ongrills' (corruption of hungry hills). They used to say there was a headless horseman about there and I would fly up that piece going home. Going down into the village there was Findlow's and Holland's yards, New Grange Farms, the Fountain Inn and two cottages, and another farm, Waterhouse. They've all been knocked down and gone under the reservoir now.

In the wartime, Meerbrook School was packed with evacuees. There were curtains to divide classes. One teacher came on a bike from Leek, Miss Horton. I was terrified of her, if you were late you got put behind the blackboard. I couldn't do long division.

Our confirmation.

I remember the army camp on Blackshaw Moor being full of Americans. They would march around the roads, and sometimes pass us on our way to school. I was terrified of their massive tanks. My older sister would say "Any gum chum?" and they would give us oranges or chewing gum. And I'd be cowering behind.

Once coming out of school, we could see a barrage balloon hooked up and stuck on the Roches. The others said it would explode, so I flew for home. I remember the searchlights and being scared of the planes going over. One crashed in the woods at Upperhulme.

I went to Meerbrook school until I was eleven, then caught a bus from the village into Milner School, Leek until I was fourteen. I didn't want to leave, I liked going to school.

We stayed off school at times to help Mum when they were harvesting at home. I remember once they were cutting corn with scythes in the meadow below the hayshed. It had rained on it and it had gone flat. We also stayed off at threshing time.

Everything was hard work, there was no electric till I left home. The earth closet was across the yard, Dad had to clean it out with a barrow. There was a black lead grate with a boiler and tap on one side, and an oven with rings on top. The grate started to come out, so we had to put bricks under it to hold it in.

Mum had a bag of flour, she made her own bread. It was kept upstairs, and mice would sometimes get in it. So you'd creep upstairs and clap your hands on the bag and hopefully kill them, then pick them up by their tails, carry them downstairs and throw them on the fire. And you'd cure your own bacon and hams and hang them in the kitchen. I've seen maggots in them, but we ate them and we're still here aren't we? They make all this fuss nowadays. That bacon melted in your mouth.

And we made butter, but I only liked it fresh. Eggs we put in steens with waterglass (isinglass) to preserve them when there was a glut, and to see through the moult at the start of the winter when the hens stopped laying.

At the back of the cowshed where the 'sok' drained out and ran, it had grassed over. I was playing round there one day, and I thought I could walk on it, and I went in up to my waist. I was screaming and Dad came running to see what was wrong. He pulled me out and had to put me in the brook to clean me up. I must have stunk something awful.

I was always in trouble, I should have been a boy. We used to go and play with Smiths next door, and my older sister set some gorse bushes on fire and ran off. They always thought I'd done it. When we were older, my younger sister had a firework one night in the bedroom. I suppose it would be a banger. She was playing round a candle with it when it caught. She had to get across the room, over the bed and throw it through a little window quickly. It went off as it fell. We'd flown in bed, pretending to be asleep, when Dad came rushing in "What the bloody hell's going on!"

We slept three in a bed, I was in the middle because I was always cold. In the war, we had an evacuee lad who worked for us, and he slept in a bed across the bottom of our bed.

Prisoners of war came and drained our Top Field with shovels, yes all by hand . It was moor then, and when Tatton's chimney was at Upperhulme, we had clinker from there and filled in over the pipes with that. Dad did a lot of work up there, and he was also a good drystone waller.

We went to chapel Sunday school for a while, then to church most weeks. There were lots of classes, and exams. I've got prizes and a Roger Morris Bible. We went in the choir too, and sometimes played on the bell, it's a wonder we didn't go up to the ceiling. Then there were the camp meetings at Folly Rest. I loved the music, Hollinsclough Band. We sat on straw bales under the hayshed, and there was tea and cakes in the house.

In the meadow below the farm, we grew crops, kale or turnips. We ploughed it with horses. I remember turnip thinning, hard work but I liked it, and hogging them up after lifting. At the top of the field a lot of docks grew, and when I got older I liked books, so if I wanted to be on my own, I'd hide in the docks with a book and an old coat to lie on.

When I left school I had to go out to work, we couldn't all stay at home. My sister was there and Ephraim and Eric Docksey helped Dad to milk the cows. We sent about ninety gallons of milk. So I went to work for Billy Hine at New Grange. I lived in with them for eighteen months, helping to look after the children, with housework and looking after the hens. Then I went to work in the District Bank in Derby Street, Leek in the house part as a nanny. I lived in there for five years. It was a beautiful house with a huge garden, but very cold in winter. There would be maids there before me who would have slept in the attics; and butlers and pantry butlers.

When my older sister left home to get married, I went back. I didn't like going between the cows, and so I didn't like milking. That was hand milking, then Dad got an engine and units to milk with. I used to look after the hens, and there were a lot, and I used to deal with the sheep. I remember for sheep washing we had to shut the lambs in the stable and walk the ewes down to the Churnet at Abbey Green, it must be two miles there. Then wash them, then walk them back. I'll not forget the noise when we got back, the bleating of the ewes and lambs when they were let back together.

Ploughing, up Gun.

The first year I went home, we still had just horses. It would be 1954 because it was a wet summer, it never stopped raining. You couldn't make hay, and we never did finish. Anyway Dad bought a Fordson tractor from Cundy's at Folly Rest. No one would drive it, we'd never had any vehicles before. There was only me who'd get on it, and we were on a bank behind the farm; I was steering it, I hadn't a clue about gears or any thing, so I'd got it in the wrong gear and it reared up. I think they were known for it. My brother George was on the trailer, they were forking hay up to him, and my Dad was swearing and going mad, they thought I should be able to manage it. We had to fetch Eric from another field to sort it out. Eric looked after the horses, and even shod them. He was very strong.

I'd help Mum with the housework. Monday was washday, it would take all day with boiler, dolly tub and mangle. Tuesday you could be mending and darning socks. Thursday was bedroom day, sweeping out and shaking mats. There was no telly, but we had a wind-up gramophone. When I was cleaning upstairs sometimes I'd put it on and work faster to

WI trip to Wedgwood 1960

Front Row: May Clowes, May Burgess, Vinnie Clulow, Mrs Nicholson, Mary Rider, Rhona Bennison, Vera Day

Second row: Harriet Barks, Nelly Barks, Louie Machin, Mary Day

Third row: Gladys Hine, Elsie Taylor, Fanny Pimlott, Mrs Walmsley, Alice Mellor, Sarah Turnock

Back Row: Miriam Robinson, Hilda Allen, Winnie Hine, Edna Barlow, Gertie Brooks, Mary Hine, Mrs Foster, Lucy Hine

Meerbrook School Late 1930s

Frank Carter, Bill Hine, George Swindlehurst, Charlie Robinson, George Mellor, Jack Shepherd, Ron Allen, Tom Hine
Ms Clowes, Mabel Belfield, Marjorie Bowers, Mary Gibson, Frances Gibson, Gladys Hine, Mary Robinson, Cissie Hine, Mary Plant, Alice Hine
Ms Beaumont, Dorothy Carter, Evelyn Smith, Edna Plant, Elizabeth Turnock, Mary Gibson, Elsie Robinson, Freda Taylor
Jessica Cundy, Elizabeth Robinson, Jean Plant, Dorothy Robinson, Sylvia Ryder, Phylis Beardmore
Nancy Semple, John Swindlehurst, Ken Ryder, Wilf Hine, Cliff Belfield, Louie Machin.

Dr McClew's wife with a baby at Gunside.

it. There'd be Gracie Fields records. Then there was ironing. You put your iron in the fire to heat it, sometimes getting some coal tar on your clothes, so you had to rub it with soap and hopefully get it off. Your iron soon went cold.

When Mr Grove was at the vicarage, we did half a day there on a Thursday, scrubbing steps and floors and getting coal in. That was me or my sisters as we left school.

Mum went to a furniture sale in Leek and bought us girls some bikes. We had to walk to Leek to fetch them. Nobody would have the old Raleigh bike but me, it had no three speed and flat tyres, so I had to walk home with it. We learned how to ride them in the meadow in front of the house. Betty went straight into a gutter, full of trees, but she came out alright. We were hopeless to start with but eventually we got going. We went everywhere on them, even to dances. We used to love the dances, there were a lot of young people in the village then. The men would congregate at the top end of the village hall. They had to go outside round the back to spend a penny, there were no proper toilets, only an old Elson for the ladies. I think the band would sometimes get a waft from that. The men would go down to the pub for a while sometimes, women didn't go in pubs then.

We once went to a dance at the Tenants' Hall, at Swythamley. It was beautiful, all the animal heads on the walls, and a massive log fire. When we came out someone had taken my front light and my bike pump. I was so mad about it, I had to follow the others over Gun, but they could go faster than me with their three speeds. Half way down Gun I tipped over, but I got back home just about in one piece. You had to creep past Mum and Dad's bed to get in our room, but I bet they heard us.

Then next morning I had to get on my bike and be back at the Bank House in Leek by 7.00 am when I lived in. I never found out who pinched my stuff. We didn't go out much, but we always enjoyed ourselves. Of course you hadn't much money. When I started at the Bank House I got fifteen shillings a week, and it went up to one pound and ten shillings when I finished. I could have gone on a machine in a mill for more money, but Mum and Dad wanted me to go home for a while, until I was married and moved to Buttyfold Farm.

Meerbrook Church
was rebuilt in
1873. The architect
was Richard
Norman Shaw.

Right: The old church and its tower
which were built in 1538.

Below: Gunside Farm.

Minnie Findlow

I was born at Hulme Walfield, near Congleton in September 1914. Later we moved to Swettenham village for a while. My dad, Tom, worked for his father on the farm. That was Home Farm, Swettenham. Mum had come from Bournemouth. She had lost her first husband with pneumonia after being married for only two years, and told us that she was a widow for thirteen years before marrying Dad. She was a servant for some people who moved up from Bournemouth to Swettenham Hall; and while there she met and married Dad. I remember going to Congleton Market with my Granny and Grandad on the pony and trap. I thought I was the bee's knees.

We moved to Roche Grange in 1923, renting it from 'Bossy' Lomas. He was a character. Then after about two years we moved to the Middle farm.

I walked the two miles to school wearing clogs, and if I wasn't back by a certain time, my Dad would come looking for me. We'd a lot of hens then, and I had to go round feeding them and collecting eggs when I got back from school, else there was a row. I was also made to walk to Sunday school, twice sometimes. Mum went to church regularly, but Dad was chapel, so they went to special services at chapel, like the harvest.

I started milking when I was twelve; we milked about eighteen cows. The milk went into Nestlé's churns. Sometimes Dad helped Abraham Taylor at Newsett, so he took our churns down, loaded them together with theirs and picking other churns up on the way, took them on to Crooked Chimney on the Macclesfield road to meet the Nestlés wagon. We also kept some sheep and had to walk them over the hill and down to the river Dane to wash them.

About 1926 or 1927 they had foot and mouth at next door Roche Grange. Heapys were there then. And even though it is only a stone's throw away, we never got it, nor the other farm; yet across the fields less than a mile away at Pheasants Clough where Browns lived, they had it. Heapys never knew where it came from. The cattle were all killed and burnt. There was no compensation then, it was terrible. After that, they went from there, I think it finished them. We had disinfectant at the gate. Dad was worried sick.

Frank Stonier worked for us, and I remember one Saturday night working at the barn down by the Meadows. The ten acre meadow was ready for haycarting and there was only the two of us to do it. My Dad was off work for some time with rheumatic fever and others were busy with their own hay. I was only fourteen and we'd had to do all the other work first, milking and everything. It was all pitchfork work and it got to one o'clock in the morning; Frank was putting the hay through the pitchhole to me and I was levelling it. I was so tired, I said "I can't do any more, we'll have to leave it." He was a strong man and his reply was "They't eether ave shift it or bloody smother in it." What would they say nowadays? Well, when we'd finished that load I said, "I'm not doing any more, I just can't." Next day was Sunday and Dad wouldn't let us work. So it had to wait till Monday and luckily the weather held.

My husband Jack had lived just up the fields at Buxton Brow. We'd met after a do at Meerbrook, a dance I think. I would go down to the dance with Winnie and Elsie Taylor from Newsett, down the road. You had to be back by a certain time, so I'd go back with them to there, then go on myself. I used to go like fury when I'd left them. Then this night I heard someone come behind me and I went faster than ever; I was frightened, but it turned out to be Jack. He'd been to the dance too.

Sheep washing. Tom Skerratt is standing on the right.

Clarence Findlow, Joe Clulow, George Bailey and a young Les Findlow at the Fountain.

We were married and lived with Mum and Dad for a while. Our son Les was born and when he was eighteen months old we moved to the Fountain Inn down in Meerbrook village. Mr and Mrs Parker, who were at Roches Hall, owned it and we rented it off them. She was known as Gran Parker and was the housekeeper there. Mum and Dad stayed on at Roche Grange for a while then moved to Yew Tree Farm, Gratton for a few years; then Mum was taken ill, so they had a sale and moved to Denford near Longsdon. She died two years later, and Dad came to live with me.

When Jack had left school, he worked for his uncle Ernest down in Bearda Hollow. It was a joinery and wheelwright business. Jack made wooden gates and got seven shillings and sixpence a day which was a lot of money for a teenage lad then. But he had to make so many a day for that.

When we went to the Fountain he put a big wooden shed up at the bottom of the ground and worked in there. And George Mellor from the Lea came from school and worked with him. We'd also got six cows, a few pigs and some hens. We sold the milk. I never went out at all; at weekends I'd do extra cooking and cater for people who passed by. The water had to be fetched from the well. There was no electric, it was all parafin lamps, you had to fill them every day, they were hung on the wall. It was hard work. You never got to bed till after midnight, you had to wash glasses; we daren't leave them till morning with having children.

We'd start at about six in a morning. Jack milked the cows and jobs like that then would go to work for eight o' clock. I had to clean up, fill the lamps, see to the children, get the food, do the pigs and hens and be ready to open up at ten thirty. People would soon start coming in, it was pretty busy. We did well there, I do admit. Jack would serve at night when he'd finished work. The beer came in wooden barrels from Marstons. I think it went to Stoke station, then to Leek station, then it was fetched with horse and cart. We served the beer in jugs on the bar into glasses or beer mugs. I didn't enjoy it much, it was such hard work; but Jack did, he never wanted to leave.

When my youngest son Eric was born and you had to stay in bed in those days, the Hine twins from Wetwood came to help, a week each.

In the middle Church Cottage lived old Joe Clulow and his wife. He was a drinker and he'd come in of a morning. Later his wife would come and peep round the door "Where is he?" She'd catch hold of the scroft of his coat and drag him out, "Come on you old bugger" This would be in the afternoon and he'd be drunk. He'd told her he was going down the garden.

Fred Ward and his wife lived in the bottom cottage at that time, opposite the well. There was a pump then, that was the drinking water. One day I was fetching some water when all of a sudden there comes a saucepan of burnt potatoes out across the road. She'd let them burn and he was so savage he'd slung them across the road. I shouted "Hey Fred, what you doin' with them, you nearly hit me!" He was ever so done that I'd seen it.

Then there was Maud Armitt. She had been at Marsh Farm, and lived at the old Ivy Cottage, near where the new ones are now. She was a big lady, a real character, some didn't get on with her, but she was alright with us. She had the field which we bought off her to build Marsh View. When her brother died, he was buried at Onecote, and she said to my husband, "When I die Jack, that's where I want go; an if ther's neow money left fer tak me theer, thee mun drag me theer on a sledge."

At Buxton Brow - Jack Findlow on the right.

The Fountain in the late 1950s.

At the Fountain again.

Minnie with baby Les, at Roche Grange.

Minnie's niece Dorothy Done with Les.

Meantime Jack built Marsh View. We moved in 1939. We'd had the Fountain for four years. George and Nancy Bailey took it on; people called him Lloyd George Bailey. He'd worked with Dad at Swettenham and had come up with us to Meerbrook and stayed. He met his wife, who lived at Upperhulme and worked at the dyeworks.

We moved our stuff on a handcart down the road from the Fountain to Marsh View. I pulled Eric behind us in the pram. Anything big, Jack and George carried it down. He took the shed down and moved it, and put a big saw and an engine in it; and built a brick shed to work in. That was the start of J. L. Findlow and Sons.

When we were at Roche Grange, Dad and some neighbours, Mr Belfield from Brownsett, Stephen Hine, Mr Lomas, five or six of them would play cards; nap, a bit like poker, five cards in a hand for money. That was their hobby, they'd play for hours at a time, going to different houses. They'd play in a shed at the vicarage, the vicar liked cards, that was vicar Hadfield. He married us. He was a right'un, never seemed to

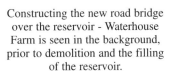

Constructing the new road bridge over the reservoir - Waterhouse Farm is seen in the background, prior to demolition and the filling of the reservoir.

bother about anything much, happy go lucky. He got on well with people, but seemed to let the church go a bit. It was in poor repair when Mr Grove came and he raised a lot of money and got things repaired. Some people liked him, some didn't, he was blunt. We always got on alright with the Groves. My lads were in the choir then. They were very good to me when we were at Marsh View. I had to go into the Cottage Hospital and have a lump removed from my breast. They took me in, took my clothes home and washed them and fetched me out. Mrs Grove was taken bad some years later and I paid her back, helping at the vicarage.

Mr Grove loved rook and crow shooting with Dad in the fields. He'd have me making rook pie. I thought it was awful when he started me doing that, but he said, "Minnie, I think you'll find it's very good" and they were. The rooks had to be young, just leaving the nest. You used the breast and the best part of the leg; pluck them, cut the meat off, cook it, then make a pie of it. He loved it! My Dad lived with us at Marsh View for twenty eight years after Mum died and Mr Grove liked to come down and talk with him. We had a budgie which talked, and Dad learned it things he shouldn't. Vicar Grove came one day and they were talking when he said "What did that bird say Tom?" Dad replied "I wasn't listening, I just missed it" It was bugger, bugger, bugger!

I remember in the 1947 winter we walked to Leek over walls, hedges and ditches and never saw them. Jack made a big sledge, and would go up to the Three Horseshoes on Blackshaw Moor to meet the bread vans; then fetch the bread back to the village, all by hand. Les Holland went with him sometimes. One of our lads wanted to go with him, but he wouldn't let him. It was that cold, with the wind you couldn't imagine it.

We were at Marsh View for twenty-one years. We left on November 4th 1959 after we'd been compulsory purchased by the Water Board to make Tittesworth Reservoir larger. It was awful. Jack along with others had fought against it for some time. The worry of it made him ill; our doctor said it was the start of the illness that killed him. We'd built our house and business up, put all we had into it, and they didn't even give us what it was worth. You had to take their price. Everyone who was affected was devastated. We moved to Ladderedge, but we'd bought the Tanyard in Leek for £1800 the year before. It was an old mill with the windows out, and water running underneath it. So we set about making that into our new yard, and my sons and grandsons run it to this day.

The Church gate.

Wilde's lorry at Brownsett.
Len Turnock, George Belfield, Ben Wilde,
Leigh Belfield and Norman Belfield.

Frank Belfield at Hurdlow, late 1930s.

Minnie Findlow at Marsh View.

At Brownsett, Leigh and Norman Belfield.

Two photographs of the Teapot Club at Flash Bar.

Annie Potter

I was born in 1914 at Cocket Knowl on Turn Edge, Quarnford. My Mum was Suzanna Mellor from Cocket Knowl, Dad was Jim Bratt. He was born in a cottage known as Reowbub Cassle (Rhubarb Castle), Upperhulme. I think its gone now, it would go under the factory, when it expanded. My Grandad Joe worked in the dyehouse and they moved up to the Homestead, and he farmed as well. Dad worked in the dyehouse, dyeing silk, and stayed with his parents, only coming back to us at weekends. I had a brother and two sisters, James was the oldest, then Nelly, then me, then Gwen. I remember us girls taking an envelope with the rent in for the Homestead to Miss Mellor, a posh old woman who lived in a cottage above Far Brook. She gave us tea and some pineapple.

When me Dad were a kid, John Hall was at Roches Hall, and one day Dad and Aunty Annie were up Roche road and John Hall comes up with his horse and trap, and the gate was shut. So dad opened it for him, and he reached in his pocket and gave dad a penny and a sixpence. Well Dad wouldn't be much age, and he looked at the sixpence and thought "This little thing's no good" and slung it and kept the penny. He went down and told his Mum - she wouldn't be very pleased.

Grandad taught in the Sunday school at Upperhulme chapel, reading the bible and the like. If a child said, "Please Mr Bratt, what's this word?" he'd reply; "Eeh, I dunna know, call it Manchester."

At Cocket Knowl, Granny Mellor lived with us. She was a good old woman, like a midwife, she'd go out to people, they'd fetch her. Old Dr Hazlewood would be going to somebody and he'd stop at Cockett Knowle and call "Is Liza there? Come on Liza, follow me" And no matter what the weather me Gran had got her jacket on and was going. She was there when a lot were born. The doctor were a rum fellow, but very well thought of. Me mother would hate him coming because he would jump off his horse and say "Just hold it" to her. Well it was never still, it was that lively. It once trod on mother's big toe and it never did go right.

Granny went to Nield Farm, near Flash when both girls were born, Madge and Gladys Wood. She'd go to them and maybe stay over for a day. The first time she went they hadn't got much to eat in, so she says to Jim, their Dad, "Go up Flash Bar shop and get summat eat." So off he went, and what d'you think he came back with? A donkey stone! So me Granny says, "They cost ave that, an I'm gooin wom."

Jim had a parlour with no furniture in, and he built a hencote in there. Then he says "Ow am I gooin't get it ight." So he made a little ladder, and took a pane out of the window and the hens would run up the ladder and go in. Ey, he did have some eggs though. He used walk to Leek Market with them.

I liked being at Cocket Knowl; there were two or three red peonies in the garden on the front, and a lilac tree at the bottom end. Then a lilac tree below on that garden and a hencote. We kept three cows and made some butter. There'd be a stirk or two, and perhaps a young calf; a fat pig and some hens. We had to manage on our own; and you could get some shocking bad weather. Eeh, snow! You could only see the chimneys and roof of houses sometimes. You just had to manage as long as you'd got some flour in. You had to rid to get to the coal.

J. P. Joule, a butcher from Buxton, would come and kill a fat calf and take it. My brother Jim once thought he was big enough to watch, but he soon came running when its head was cut off. Then there was Tommy Goodwin, a pig butcher who lived at Hawks Nest. He'd wrap a pig's eye up in a bit of paper and give it to you for a toffee. We'd squeal and run off.

There was a bit of a shop at Barber's at Back o' th' Cross. If you ran short of stuff you went there. You could get a loaf, or sugar or corn. And you could get lots of things at Flash Bar shop, but that was a longer walk. Emmie Hodgkinson kept that. Mr Barber, and Mr Goodwin at Manor Farm down in Gradbach had horse and traps, and went to Macclesfield on Saturdays. So if you badly needed anything they'd get it for you and you fetched it when they got back. They were good neighbours, Mr Goodwin was grand; he taught us at Sunday School at Gradbach Chapel on a Sunday afternoon. I'd go with Ethel Brunt from Back o' th' Cross. She lived with her Grandma, old Peggy Brunt. My sister went to Flash Church, but I liked to go chapel, down the fields and over the brook.

Now Mr Sigley from Mill Cottage was a hard man. He grew watercress, and every Saturday he'd take it with a pushbike and box to Macclesfield Market. They'd be queued up for it. And it was uphill all the way to Allgreave. His lads, Joseph William and Laurence helped him up the hill. He fetched coal from Pennyhole pit at Three Shires Head with a handcart. When it was full, they had to haul it up through Knotbury to Flash, then downhill to Gradbach. A long way; Billy in front, and Laurie pushing behind. They wouldn't be that old and if they got tired he'd kick their backsides. I remember me Grandad Mellor would fetch coal from Pennyhole, I can see him now with his legs bagged up to th' knees, 'cause it was that wet and they were on their knees hiking it out. He was gone all day.

Mr Wilkinson came to Hawks Nest. He was chauffeur to Gentleman Beswick who lived at Northfield House in Flash. He was a rum old card. He did so like his beer. I think he came from Manchester and he'd walk over to Cocket Knowl. He was a torment; mother was lookin' to things outside once and he took teapot lid off and put it in kettle. Well me mother blamed us kids for this lid goin' missin' but we'd no idea where it was. Then about a week later she found it and said, "Its that damned Wilkie!" After a while, he went to live at Northfield House; his wife did the housekeeping. She was a lovely woman; he spent nearly all his time in the New Inn. They asked him when he was sober how he went on driving for Gentleman Beswick. He said, "Aye, I always see three roads, and I keep up the middle one." He was very likeable.

I went to Flash school. It took about half an hour to get there. I should have gone to Ramshaw for a fortnight before I left school, when we'd moved to Shaw Bottom, but I didn't. We had to take a cup and go up to the well if we wanted a drink. The Market was on about once a month, Tommy Mottram's one time, Bagshaws from Buxton another, a month in turn. It was nice to go to school on Market day; you could hear 'em shouting and bidding. The teacher was always after you because you were trying to listen to the market instead of doing your work. Every now and then you stood on your form to have a look through the window. You were in trouble if you were caught.

The teacher in the big class was Mr Sparks. I had to take him half a dozen eggs from my mother every week. In the small class, the teacher was Miss Beswick from the Travellers Rest. She'd come, when it was snowing, with her gaiters on, and put them on the fireguard to dry. Jack Beswick was gamekeeper. He'd fetch you off Ramshaw Rocks if he saw you where you shouldn't be. He was a good gamekeeper; they were nice folks. And Flash had its own policeman then, Bobby Foster, he'd two daughters, Rose and Edna. And I think after that Bobby Rowley, a big ginger-haired fellow. He lodged with Mrs Mellor at Top o' Morridge.

Then of course there was Tea Pot Club. That was on the third Monday in June. We had to be up early, it would be a busy day, a lot of people gathered there then. We had new socks and shoes and a white hat because it was always a fine day, or seemed to be. We had some very nice days anyway. Mother had to go early because those who'd been getting ready and making fires and doing, would be wanting tea brewing, perhaps as early as eight o' clock. She helped in the chapel room, under the chapel with the refreshments and washing up. It wasn't very high in that room but they used it before they had a village hall. There was a kitchen with stoves, they cooked great pieces of meat and boiled hams. You could have a hot dinner, and there were great slabs of cake. People came in all day for butties and cake.

There'd be two bands playing, it could be Buxton Band, Hollinsclough Band or Burbage Silver Band. Some of them 'ud be drunk as monkeys later on. And there'd be a few stalls selling bits of stuff. And I remember donkeys, did they come from Longnor? There'd be gettin' on for ten of 'em. That was something, a donkey ride, from Flash over to the post office, else down the new road to Ernie Beswicks. The pubs were going all day, there were some merry times, kids playing all day; it was the highlight of our year. But we had to go back in good time; Mum had jobs to see to at home and Gran was getting older. There'd be a dance at the New Inn up in the Club Room. Fred and Bessie Wardle kept the New Inn, and his brother Jack Wardle kept the New Inn at Upperhulme, which is now The Rock.

We moved to Goldsitch Moss and then to Shaw Bottom as time went on, it was nearer to Dad's work and he came home then. When we lived on the Moss, if there came a heavy thunderstorm, when it had dried up, Mum would send us onto the shale hillocks for coal. You soon got a good bucketful, you could see it easily, it was that bright; and it burnt well. Joe Newton, a baker from Buxton came round on a Wednesday with bread; and J. P. Joule and Frank Simpson, butchers came on Fridays and Saturdays. We kept a horse then and I remember fetching corn on horseback from Back o' th' Cross. And we went to Mrs Slack to have our clogs and shoes mended.

I left school at thirteen and went to help Aunty Annie Parker at Roches Hall. Brocklehursts owned it, Aunty Annie was housekeeper and Uncle Jim did odd jobs. Tattons would come to stay in summer, Mrs Tatton and the girls, sometimes with guests, sometimes Mr Max Tatton. They'd come most days, sometimes staying over. I helped with cooking and washing up, staying for six months. Aunty looked after Captain Courtney Brocklehurst when he was up there. She said he was very nice, he was no trouble. She'd ask him what he wanted for tea, he'd say "Don't bother about me, Mrs Parker; just put me some bread and cheese, I'll be alright." He was an outside man, always out on the Roches or somewhere. Uncle Jim blessed his menagerie, he kept emus, llamas, wallabies, a yak, I don't know what else. I well remember going down one Sunday, and going with Uncle Jim

The Beswick family.

Left: Jack Beswick, gamekeeper.

Below:
1940s up at Flash Bar.
Front Row:
Ray Kirkham, Barney Bamford (reporter)
Back Row: Jim Beswick, Tommy Wardle,
Fred Wardle, Jack Beswick Snr, Jack
Beswick Jnr, Arthur Smith.

The Beswick family, two Jims and two Johns, outside The Traveller's Rest, Flash.

Outside Flash Bar shop.

Probably a gamekeeper at Flash Bar.

feeding the emus with a bucket. Everything was loose and you had to watch where that bloody old yak was. It tipped the coalman over once. Uncle Jim said to me, "Luk thee wench, I hant a button." They'd pecked all his buttons off.

Uncle Jim had a little old Austin car, and Captain Brocklehurst had a big green Bentley, it would roar away, you could hear it go all across Blackshaw Moor. Uncle Jim said, "They't none get mey in theer!" But one Saturday morning the Captain asked uncle to go to Leek with him, and he plucked up courage and got in saying, "Now then, they't got goo steady." Well, going round Bennisons at Tittesworth, it blew uncle Jim's hat off, and he said "By Gyad, if ever ah get ight er 'ere, ah'm none gettin' in agen!" I think they had a job getting' 'im home.

Captain Brocklehurst was different from his brother, Sir Philip was more stand offish; I suppose it was his position. He was coming across the back of the Roches on his horse one day, and our Jim was coming down to Shaw Bottom and sees him coming along. He'd be about twelve at that time. Sir Philip pulls up to the gate and says to Jim, "Open the gate." Course if the gates weren't too big he'd jump them. Anyway Jim took no notice. "Are you deaf lad? Open the gate." Again no notice. "Are you going to open the gate?" Jim said, "If you please," and Sir Philip said, "Oh, sorry."

Jim would've sat on that stile all day he said if Sir Philip hadn't said sorry; and he chanced his luck considering Sir Philip was our landlord at Shaw Bottom. He was alright to live under though. If your windows needed painting up, you'd go down Swythamley and fetch paint or nails. Kids were sent to fetch stuff. I well remember my Dad sending me to the Hall. Sir Philip had a monkey and I was terrified of going, but I never saw it in the end. Then having to walk right back, up by Clough Head. It was heavy; I'd be thirteen. And they'd have rent day dances, tea and a dance. I went to one do in summer, it was a good feed, and packed out. Sir Philip came in later on in the night and mixed with everyone.

Up there we went to Newstone chapel, you could hear the cattle in the shippon next door. I remember Vernon Egerton and cousin Arthur Clowes preaching there when they were young. And we'd still go to special services at Gradbach. Mrs Dale sometimes preached, and it was very rare then for a woman to preach. We'd sing the hymn, "O for a thousand tongues to sing," and she'd say after, "Isn't that a lot of tongues." She was a grand woman.

Mr Gilman, the packman came round every so often. He lived in Flash and only had one arm. In his pack he'd have pieces of cut cloth, needles, thimbles and all such like.

And I remember Edward Ash who carved the pulpits in Flash and Meerbrook churches. They are the same but Meerbrook has a butterfly on, and Flash a mouse. They moved from Farbrook to Top House, Flash. Their son Teddy Oakes Ash went school when I did, and there were three girls, Olive, Kathleen and Jean.

Another old character was owd Lazarus Belfield from Buxton. He was a hen dealer, and he'd go from Burbage to Leek Market every Wednesday with a pony and flat cart with hen crates on. And they'd always have a drink or two. He had two or three sons, Jim was a coalman, Phil kept a pub in Buxton. When he got back from Leek, he'd be drunk and so go to bed, leaving the lads to pluck and draw the hens. They could be working a lot of the night. Then the dressed poultry would be ready for Lazarus to take round the hotels in Buxton early next morning.

One time the lads were going on a trip to London, and they took old Laz with them. Old Laz always bragged that everyone knew him, so one of the lads tipped a little shoe black and said to him, "Thee seys that owd chap over theer, go an say to 'im, Well if tha isn't Lazarus from Buxton." Which he did. Owd Lazarus thought that were grand, "I teowd yer, I teowd yer, I'm known everywheer!"

After working at Roches Hall, I went into the dyeworks at Upperhulme, winding, coneing or purning. Sammy Wood took the stuff away with a traction engine and a big trailer. They called him Sammy Tractor. I was there for years; it wasn't good pay but it was work near to home. If we wanted to go out we had to walk to Flash, there'd sometimes be a dance at Flash Bar; the 'Forresters' had put a hut up. On Club Feast day there'd be a dance there as well as at the New Inn. It would be where you met your future husband, there wasn't much else. Sometimes on a Sunday we'd sit against Gibsons at Middle Hills and watch for cars to go past. There weren't many then. There were motor bikes. Lads from Flash would go down to the Three Horseshoes on Blackshaw Moor. George Tunnicliffe kept it. It would be cram full Saturday night and Sunday, some would be too drunk to go home; perhaps George would let them sleep in a building.

There were some characters at the dyeworks. Owd Joe Clulow worked in the black dyehouse. He'd drink at night and fall out all day with his fellows. One day he said to little Alec Pickford, "I'll tell thee what Alec; if tha had but had a teel, tha'd a bin grandest little monkey that ever clumb a trey." And Alec once said back, "If they liv'st ferever Cluler, they't ave dey sumtime!" And the story goes that when owd Joe died, his wife went to see the vicar about his funeral, and the vicar asked, "Where do you think he's going to go?" And she replied: "Why Heaven of course, Hell's full of parsons like they!"

The Dyehouse at Tattons.

Upperhulme Mill after the fire, 1891.

Some of the early employees.

Employees at Tatton's Upperhulme Mill, early 1900s.

Winning first prize at Leek Market.

Eric and Arnold Moss

Marjorie Moss

I was born at Fold Villa, Leekfrith. Mum and Dad were Fred and Gertie Robinson and I have a sister Muriel. We went to school in Leek, West Street school then Brittania Street. We usually walked to school, but sometimes we'd get a lift in our Dad's cattle wagon when he was taking a few sheep or cattle into the butcher's abattoirs in Leek. There were three, one in Pump Street, Sidney Bailey's in Belle Vue and Sammy Bostock's in Cross Street. Dad would supply several butchers with stock, Mr Ash always wanted a cow heifer, the nicest meat, more tasty than these modern animals. Then there was Mr Godwin in St Edward Street and Mr Reg Pointon in Heywood Street. The cattle would be Shorthorns or Angus, mainly heifers.

When we left school we worked at home on the small farm. It was only ten or twelve acres, then in 1950s Dad bought some extra land. Dad would go to markets, first Banbury, then York and in later years Mold. He'd be gone maybe two or three days a week, buying newly calved or in-calf dairy cows and heifers. The cattle from York came back on the train to Leek Station, where Muriel and me would have to walk them back from. Enza Barks worked at the Station, in the Goods office where we had to sign for the cows. Sometimes we'd have one wagon load, sometimes two, maybe twenty cattle.

They were always hungry after their train ride, and I remember it was hard work keeping them off the "Rec" when the iron railings had been taken away during the war. We walked them up Burton Street, of course that's all built up now, down Belle Vue, through Abbey Green, then when we got to Villa Road we'd let them graze on the wide verges. Some farmers would come to meet us there, take a look at the cows first and perhaps pick the best out to buy. We sold all the cattle from home, people bought one or two. Most only kept twenty odd cattle, if that. Mr Felthouse at Lower Haddon had off us. He had a fancy horse and a fancy cart, and was gone to Leek every Wednesday morning by 9.30.

We went to a lot of the farms in Meerbrook and the surrounding area with Dad, taking cows. I remember going up to Ginny Riley's, at Thornyleigh Green, I'll never forget Ginny, she was a character. There were lots of gates on the way up there, and Dad hadn't got very good brakes on the wagon, or so he said, and he wouldn't stop for us, we had to run on and get in the wagon as it was going, after opening each gate. We went up there many a time. We used to go to Horse Haylands, Clowes at Greenhouse, Parnell, Beardmore's at Newhouse. Nearly everyone had cows off us regular. Up Gun to Old Hay Top, we'd walk them down to the farm with Mrs Belfield and Master. He'd come to buy heifers off Dad and we'd tie his bike on the back of the cattle wagon to go back.

We didn't sell milk ourselves, we had to make cream and butter, turning the separator by hand not electric. That's why my shoulders are bad, and with wheeling heavy barrows. We had friends and customers who had a bit of cream and butter off us. We didn't make a lot, it might have been weekends not every day, depending on what cows we'd got in.

I remember Mr and Mrs Charles Dale being at Lower Foker Farm, before they went to Rudyard Hall. They'd go to Leek with a horse and cart, and we'd have a lift back with them on a Wednesday from school. Then there were Baileys at Upper Foker. I remember Edie loading hay on a cart after it was pitched to her. Her brother Jim was struck by lightning in the yard when he was young, but luckily he got over it. I never knew their Mum, she must have died young.

We never went out much, Dad wouldn't let us socialise, just go to markets with him. Except we went to special services at Meerbrook Chapel, like the anniversary or the harvest. We'd go with the Baileys. And the Camp Meetings at Cundy's at Folly Rest. We enjoyed that, under the hayshed, with different preachers and a band. There were a lot of people went there.

I remember Jabez Mellor from The Lea at Meerbrook. He was the lengthsman who did our piece of road. He used to leave his barrow, brush and shovel at our place. He'd clear all the sludge and leaves up, down the road from Folly Rest, up Villa Bank and across Villa Road, past Villa field to where the Rural met the Town. He used to clear it all up lovely with his barrow, and leave his pile outside the Villa past the gate. He kept the culverts and ditches clear to get the water off the roads. He had a tea can and he'd get Mum to brew him a can of tea.

When fuel was rationed in the war, you had to fill forms in to show where stock were to be delivered to get fuel for the wagon. Later Coopers, hauliers from North Rode would bring cattle back from York; and Haydons would come back from Mold.

We didn't go markets for a while during 1947 winter, because we were snowridding. The road from the bottom of Upper Foker across to the rocks above Abbey Green never was cleared. It wasn't used much till May when all the snow melted. It went solid till you could walk on top of it. High-Up Lane stayed clear, it blew it off there. I remember Fred Smith's wagon picked milk up at the bottom of Upper Foker, and Mr Turnock from Gunside, and Mr Smith from Parkhouse came down the fields to Fould Farm, then along with Mr Elks from there, they'd come up Villa bank with their horses and milk churns to meet the wagon.

In 1948 we lost Mum, and in 1958 we lost Dad. About a month after Dad died, the calf man who dad supplied in York Market came down, and asked me and my sister if we'd go to local markets and buy calves for him. He supplied rearers and fatteners. So we did, that's how we started. We bought from Chelford and Leek, sometimes Beeston if he wanted more, and met the man halfway at Woodhead. We kept Dad's wagon, Mu drove, I didn't fancy wagon driving. If we bought at Chelford, we'd bring the calves home, unload them and feed them, then feed them next morning and take them on the Tuesday. On Wednesday, we'd meet at night time after Leek Market. Up at Woodhead about seven o' clock. I remember when the Moors murders happened, it wasn't far away, and while we were waiting for the calf man, we saw the police and they came and had a word with us. Never forget it.

We went nearly every week, it could be tricky in bad weather. One time we were late, because it was slippy. He'd gone, and we had to bring the calves back, and take them again the next day. Once it was like going through a tunnel of snowdrifts up there, it was ever so high, the wagon looked little. We never got stuck though. When we came back at night, we'd call at a fish and chip shop at Romiley and have a lovely fish. I'd pass it to Mu as she was driving. We really enjoyed it.

John Knott was the auctioneer at Chelford, and Roy Knight and Roy Middleton at Leek. In 1963 and 1965 we won the Christmas Fatstock Show at Leek Market. When we first went to the markets, some of the dealers didn't want us there and bid up for the calves we wanted. So we let them have them, and it cost them money, but we got ours eventually. We bought mainly Friesian bulls, perhaps some Angus if there was an order.

Dad always said if he'd got sons he wouldn't let them be dealers, but he never reckoned on his daughters doing it.

Bill Goodwin, Alderlea.

Thr Old Vicarage, Meerbrook.

Meerbrook School c.1930.

Two photos of haymaking at Alderlea with Mrs Goodwin loading.

Sylvia Buxton

I was born at Alderlea, Meerbrook in the 1930s; the eldest of five children. I had four brothers, and we all went to Meerbrook School. The teacher was Miss Horton; she was very, very strict, we were scared of her. The cane hung on the blackboard and if you didn't know your times tables by heart you got a rap across the knuckles with it. You had to put your hand up if you wanted to go outside to the toilet, and sometimes she didn't believe you needed to go; but when she let you go she'd snap "Don't be long!" Then when you came back, she'd say your clogs were too noisy, it was upsetting the lesson. Mum had to get rubbers put on mine, and she still said they were too noisy. Our clogs came from Biddulph and District, the supply firm, and came on the corn lorry.

I always remember that Miss Horton had bad hands, and while she was watching you in lessons, she'd be rubbing something onto her hands. I think she wore thin gloves later. On

Mrs Goodwin and Sylvia Goodwin, 1930s, with Mrs Grove in the background.

Ash Wednesday you turned up for school and went to a service in church, then you could have the rest of the day off. And woe betide you if you missed it, she threatened us. Mr Grove, the vicar asked us questions, and he seemed to ask us chapel children more than the others.

We had to fetch water from Mrs Grove's kitchen at the vicarage. Two of you went and fetched a pail full. I remember once I went, and as we passed the vicar's shed, on a line across the front was a row of rooks hanging. We called them all crows then. I was amazed and told Mum when I got home. She said "He eats them, he makes crow pie"

You could go home for dinner if you wanted to or you stayed behind. Dinners were delivered from the British Restaurant, Regent Street in Leek, where the courts were later. They were delivered by Mrs Day from Buttyfold. She would often have her daughter Hilda with her. Mrs Pickford, who kept the post office then, would make a break at lunchtime and dish up the dinner, as it was brought in canisters.

We liked to stay for dinners because if we went home we got rice pudding every day. It sometimes boiled over in the oven and was burnt and we got fed up of it. So with the war being on and soldiers being everywhere, I said to mum, "I don't like walking home, can I stay at school for dinners?" You'd see the soldiers lying in the hedgebottoms and creeping about, it was frightening for a time, but we were told not to be scared of them. Some officers used our front room at the farm once, I don't know what for. They had unusual telephones.

We all had to have a gas mask, and carry them to school, and we had gas mask drill there. We had to put them on and sit under the vicarage wall. Later on we went to the secondary modern schools in Leek, Milner Hall for girls and Mountside for boys.

We were a chapel family and always went along. There was Sunday School in the afternoon. Sam Bradbury from Bent Head started it, then Mrs Cundy came. We looked forward to Sunday School outings, the anniversary and the camp meetings at Folly Rest. That was under cover in the hayshed. Hollinsclough Silver Band would play. They had three speakers; sometimes Harry Bailey from Alstonefield, George Lowe from Rewlach, Mr Dale from Swainsmoor. The camp meetings went on for some years. They started having them at Gun End, but they didn't seem to last. You sat on a bank opposite the chapel and you'd be eaten by gnats.

Mr Barnett from Sandbach would come to take the anniversary services. He brought singers and a pianist; Walter Eaton Jones and sometimes his son. Frances Mon Jones played a harp; she came straight from the Welsh Eisteddfod. Mrs Barnett taught singing and brought some of her pupils. Mrs Rosemary Massey, from Gawsworth now, was one of her pupils, she still sings.

Gun End Chapel.

Mother would give them tea between services. There would be three sittings round the table, and after the evening service another two sittings. Some people would come from Sheffield and Chesterfield to follow Wilfred Barnett. It was a big day for us, I don't know how mother coped with all the catering. Walter Eaton Jones would have his tea first, then go back down to chapel to lead community hymn singing before the next service. The services would go on for maybe two hours, I don't know how we sat in the pews for that long.

Geoff - I'd be left to do all the washing up, no time for courting that day!

Even though we were a chapel family, Mr Grove, the vicar gave us a wedding present of a carving set, which we still have.

Fred Ward was the village postman and handyman. Dad asked him to make us a corn barrow. So he made us a very high sided, heavy one. You couldn't get it down the front of the cows in the fodderbing so you had to work from behind and you'd a job to push it. But it lasted for years, it was that big and strong. He was a good chapel man and would do repairs there. He drove a motorbike and sidecar and came to a sad end. They'd had a visitor, a lady who he took up to the bus stop on Blackshaw Moor. He left his bike on the Three Horseshoes and was seeing her over the road. He could only go slowly and a car came over the brow quickly and hit him. He was killed.

Old Post Office, Meerbrook

Centre: Arthur Armitt and
Bill Mountfort, outside the
Three Horseshoes,
Meerbrook, 1920s.

Below: Fred Ward on Gun
with Bill Goodwin's
Austin 7, 1940s.

The Hine family at North Hillswood
Front: Agnes, Grandma, Grandad, Esther, Richard
Back Row: Matilda (Tilly), Stephen, Lucy, John, Fred, Annie, Sam.

At Roche Side. Joe, Stephen, Alice, Lucy.

Agnes Stevenson

I was born on the 8th of November 1910 at Upper Green Farm, Onecote. My Dad was Stephen Hine, and his family were at North Hillswood, Meerbrook. Mum was Anna Salt from Elkstones. Mum and Dad had lived at Thorncliffe before renting the farm at Onecote, and while they were there in 1908 they lost a child, Arthur. He was six months old; one of my aunts said later that he'd been vaccinated for smallpox and it went wrong.

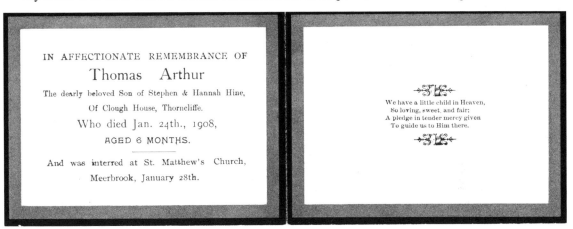

IN AFFECTIONATE REMEMBRANCE OF

Thomas Arthur

The dearly beloved Son of Stephen & Hannah Hine,
Of Clough House, Thorncliffe.

Who died Jan. 24th., 1908,

AGED 6 MONTHS.

And was interred at St. Matthew's Church,
Meerbrook, January 28th.

We have a little child in Heaven,
So loving, sweet, and fair;
A pledge in tender mercy given
To guide us to Him there.

When the first war was on, we moved to Newsett Farm, Meerbrook until 1918, when Abraham Taylor followed us in. We moved just up the field to Roche Side Farm. I can remember, in the war, my Dad walking down the road to have an examination to see if he was fit enough to go. He didn't pass though, perhaps his heart wasn't good enough. And I can remember going round the garden to the toilet at night taking a lantern with an apron over it to hide the light. I wasn't very old. When the war finished, there were celebrations at Meerbrook in Alderlea fields.

Aunty Esther and Uncle Prince Riley were at Alderlea at one time. I don't remember a lot about it; there were games and a lot of children - there were eighty children in school then. There were two teachers. We all walked, and there were no dinners, you took sandwiches. I liked school all right.

I think it was in 1918 that I lost a sister, Harriet with meningitis. She was nearly fourteen. Uncle Richard's wife had come up, and they'd all gone looking round the fields, as farmers do, except me and Harriet. When they came back, they said, "Where's Harriet?" I said, "She's gone to bed, she's got a bad head." That would be the Tuesday, and on the Wednesday morning they generally went to Leek with butter and eggs and everything. Well they didn't go, and they had the doctor, but they couldn't do anything in those days, and she died.

But that wasn't all. My brother Joe, broke out with scarlet fever, so the family weren't allowed to go to the funeral for fear of spreading it. Joe was taken to Tinsterwood Isolation Hospital, and when Mum and Dad went to see him, they could only look through a window. The nurse said he wanted some toffee, so Mum made him some. At home, someone came and "stoved" the house; I suppose it was like fumigating it. Mum and Dad had to go down the yard and gargle something, but we children didn't. Joe was the only one to get scarlet fever; it was a very sad time.

Then in 1922 Mum died of complications after childbirth. It left my Dad with six children to look after: ten day old Stephen, three year old Lucy, Annie five, Alice eight, I was eleven, the oldest girl, and Joe was fourteen and leaving school. On the morning that she died, aunty Esther was with us and she said to me, "Go down to Taylor's and see if Abraham will come and milk the cows." It was a Sunday, and he didn't get up early to take the milk; he was still in bed. But anyroad he came and milked, and I milked two or three that morning. My aunties came to wash, take turns to bake and spring clean. Aunty Esther from Golden Farm at Bradnop, Aunty Lucy from Blackshaw Moor and Aunty Tilly from Roost Hill at Bradnop. I suppose they'd walk, or come on horse and trap. Uncle Richard's wife from Lodge Farm would come up in a morning and bath the baby. Dad would warm the milk and feed him; it would be cow's milk.

Dad was very good, he could do anything. He was a good father, you couldn't have had anybody better. It must have been very hard. There were about twelve cows in milk, and young stock. He didn't sell the milk then, he made it into butter and cheese. After a while his sisters persuaded him to sell the milk and have less work, so then it was taken down to Taylors and went on their wagon. Woods from Macclesfield had some of the cheese, and Spearing's shop in Stockwell Street, Leek. You had to take it. We might have had a bit of help on a Tuesday to make butter, and later on Uncle William from Thorncliffe helped, but Dad was on his own mostly.

There wasn't much money then days, and he seemed to have bad luck with cows. If one died, it was fetched with horse and cart by Shenton's from Easing Villa at Thorncliffe. They were the knackers.

The farm was rented for some years, but then the owner wanted to sell it. Grandad told Dad to buy it. "I haven't got the money." Dad said. "You'll have nowhere to go if you don't." Grandad said. I think he helped him with the deposit. It cost £2,400 for 75 acres.

Even though we'd lost Mum, I kept going to school until I was fourteen. Then when I left I had to do all the work that Mum would have done. I remember going to Leek market with the horse and float, taking little Stephen, and standing in the Buttermarket with eggs in a basket to sell. You sometimes stood a fair while till they were sold. In the meantime, Dad went down Derby Street to the cattle market. Uncle Richard's wife stood with me for a bit sometimes, and watched the eggs if I needed to take Stephen to the toilet or anything. We put the horse up in the Wilkes Head yard.

I did all the hay loading at Rocheside -and after I got married. I milked cows from when I was eleven till I was sixty.

Dad and Joe did a garden; we had dahlias in the front border and there were blackcurrants, gooseberries and plums. I made lots of jams, pies, bread and currant bread. We kept two horses; a black, lightweight one for going to Leek, and a heavier one for mowing and the like. But they worked together grand. The light horse had a foal, and I remember getting up to look it. Mr Mountfort from Bank Top came down to say it was foaling. When I got married Dad gave me the black horse for our farm, while he broke the youngster in.

We went to chapel, Meerbrook, Gun End, Danebridge, Gradbach, even Allgreave on odd occasions. At that time there was a chapel Sunday school at Lomas's at Roche Grange. We'd go to Meerbrook Church Sunday school in the morning, then back for dinner. I remember Mum putting our Joe a pinafore over his clothes to keep his suit clean to go to chapel at Roche Grange in the afternoon. You could smell Lomas's dinner cooking because they were later having theirs. It didn't matter what the weather was, we went across the fields. Uncle George Hine was an undertaker up Ashbourne Road, and he sometimes walked up to Roche Side Sunday mornings for dinner.

When I got older, we went to dances; occasionally to Swythamley, walking through the fields with your wellingtons on, carrying your shoes under your arm and a piece of elastic round your dress to hold it out of the mud. I walked with the Brownsett girls and Minnie Skerratt. It'd be two in the morning when we got home.

I met my husband at a dance at the Three Horse Shoes on Blackshaw Moor. We got married when I was twenty-six on Easter Monday 1937. And in January 1938 Dad died suddenly. They didn't know how to tell me, I was expecting our first child. So the farm had to be sold, it made £1900 - things had gone worse by 1938. Lucy and Joe came to live with me for a while, Annie was out in service at Norton, Stephen went to Mum's cousin at Roche End for a while, then went working at Archie Day's on Blackshaw, where he ended up marrying their daughter Mary.

No, I couldn't say they were good old days, it was very hard, but you made the best of it. You could say there was more peace than nowadays.

Meerbrook School.
Annie, Agnes, Lucy, Alice.

The poet, Alfred Hine of Meerbrook.

Agnes.

My Dad, Stephen Hine, is seen 3rd from right. He used to carry Sir Philip Brocklehurst's gun on the shoots. He got 10 shillings a day, beaters 5 shillings. Above: Party of beaters and gun carriers on one of Sir Philip's shoots.

JOHN HOWARD & COMPANY LTD.

CIVIL ENGINEERING CONTRACTORS
ON ADMIRALTY, WAR OFFICE AND AIR MINISTRY LISTS

TELEPHONE : VICTORIA 8951 (8 LINES)
TELEGRAMS : HOWARDENCO, LONDON

DIRECTORS

SIR JOHN HOWARD, M.I.C.E.
RT. HON. LORD BARNBY, C.M.G., C.B.E., M.V.O.
RT. HON. LORD FAIRFAX OF CAMERON
O. T. R. LEISHMAN, M.B.E., M.I.C.E.
R. IRWIN-BROWN, B.SC., M.I.C.E.
K. M. SCOTT, F.C.A.
A. T. THORNE, B.SC., M.I.C.E.

HEAD OFFICE :

HOWARD HOUSE,
13 BUCKINGHAM GATE,
LONDON, S.W.1.

Please Reply to :

CONTRACT OFFICE :

Tittesworth Reservoir,
Nr. Leek.
Blackshaw 312.

29th June 1962.

To Whom it may concern:

TITTESWORTH DAM.

Mr. G. Collier has been employed on this contract from 1959 to 1962 and, during that time, has carried out his duties in a satisfactory manner at all times.

He was first employed as a locomotive driver on tunnel excavation on a double shift basis and then as a grout gang labourer on core wall grouting – later being made up to Ganger on this work.

During this period he became experienced in the use of Halco-Stenuick Drilling under extremely wet conditions and grouting, all of this work being very closely supervised by both the Contractor and Consultant.

As a Ganger he was responsible for night shift work and for maintaining grouting records.

I have always found him willing, co-operative and reliable, and, although he has become redundant owing to the closure of this contract, I would not hesitate to re-employ him should the occasion arise.

George Collier from Five Clouds worked as a locomotive driver at the Tittesworth Dam reconstruction.

Tittesworth Dam
reconstruction to
enlarge the reservoir
1959-1962.

Broad Lea.

Haymaking at Broad Lea, 1940. Les Holland, Jack and Vinnie Clulow,
with baby Jean, and John Clulow Snr.

Hocker Farm.

Grandad, John Poyser
Berrisford, at Hocker 1890.

Dad, Edwin Berrisford, at Hocker.

Gladys Finney

I was born at Dollards Farm, Higher Sutton, in 1920. It was a smallholding that my parents rented, and they did odd jobs for people. Mum was Prudence Downes before she was married. Dad was Edwin Berrisford; he was from a big family, one of ten children, and their homestead was Hocker Farm, near Longnor. My parents moved to Saltersford before moving back to the Hocker to look after my grandparents. It was a twenty-two acre farm, rented from the Harpur Crewe estate. In the 1930s the rent was £22. There were seven of us children, there'd been nine but Mum lost her first and last.

I remember Mum nursing Granny Berrisford. She was blind and bedridden for three years. One day she was taken ill and fell out of bed. Mum stayed with her and sent me for help. Well, I was only little and I couldn't speak - I didn't talk until I was six. I couldn't reach the door handle, I had to get a chair to stand on. But when I turned up in Oakenclough yard, Annie Phillips knew there was something wrong and came back with me to help Mum with Granny. She was a good neighbour.

We walked down the fields through Oakenclough, up Drews Hill and past Belfield House to go to Newtown school. There were twenty-eight children there then. Miss Carrington taught the infants, and Miss Hand the rest. She was very, very strict; a word out of place and you had the cane. Girls had it as much as the boys. I was running a girl round school one morning, and a cupboard door was open, and as she ran past she broke it off. So what happened to Gladys? Phyllis Ball had the cane right away, I had to wait till ten o' clock. It was the longest hour I've ever known. As soon as ten came, it was "Out Gladys!" And I had the stick. My sister, Phyllis had the cane every day one week. One day it was for playing football with the boys; another day for climbing into the churchyard and another day for climbing up a tree and getting fast because her knickers were caught up on something. I remember my future husband, Jim getting the cane for throwing a snowball through a window and breaking it. He lived at Belfield House then. One of my brothers put a drawing pin on a seat with a note saying, "He that sitteth on this shall surely rise." He was punished for that.

In 1933 there was a big snow. Everywhere was blocked and I couldn't get back home, so I stayed with my friend Dora Bradbury at Shining Ford for a week. I remember a cousin's wedding had to be postponed for a week then too. It was a smithy at Shining Ford, in normal times it was busy.

I remember old Peg Legs, who lived across Shaw Fields; he had a donkey and he was such a miserable old man. I once said to him, "Don't keep hitting that donkey." It was a good job that I was a little tich, else he would have knocked me flying with his stick. People said he was so bad tempered that he once slept out in the fields and got frostbite, and that's why he lost his legs, but I don't know if that's true. He always smoked a pipe, and he mowed Newtown churchyard with a scythe, even with his peg legs. Once he was helping someone to fall a tree. They asked him to stand back, but oh no he wouldn't. So what happened? The tree fell on him.

We went to Newtown Church and the chapel; one or the other, every week if possible. There was always a great gathering of lads round the chapel. I remember Mrs Wood from Shawfield was a very good preacher, and Walter Cundy, and an old man from Crowdicote, who had a red handkerchief sticks in my mind.

For shopping we walked to Longnor, or occasionally walked to Royal Cottage and caught a bus to Leek. And sometimes Abberlys from Rudyard would come round with a grocery van. The thing I always remember about going to Longnor, was the fighting. My brothers couldn't go without the lads down there waiting to fight them. There was no pleasure in going. I only went to Longnor Sports once. I'd be seventeen, and went to see what it was like, but it did nothing for me and I never went again.

I remember one summer night going with my cousin, Peggy Shirley for a long walk. We walked from the Hocker over to Three Shires Head, then up to Flash, back along Morridge Top to Daffodil Farm where Mrs Dale lived. She kept goats, and we had a nice cup of tea with goats milk in. Then we walked down to Hollinsclough, then took a short cut over the fields past Thick Withens and High Ash, where my Aunty Hannah and Uncle Joseph Torr lived. We reckoned it was about twenty-two miles; we enjoyed it, but we didn't go again.

When I was fourteen, I left school. My brother John worked for a cattle dealer, Jimmy Davenport, who heard of a lady wanting some help on the farm because she'd got a little girl. So I went along to Mr and Mrs Dale, at Curbishley Farm, Nether Alderley. It was a big farm, they milked thirty cows by hand. I had to start work at half past four in the morning, cleaning and washing up. I had to learn how to do things well and quickly. Mr and Mrs Dale were good employers, the food was good, but conditions were cold and hard. The workmen had nowhere to dry their clothes if they got wet. But that was the way of the world then, it was the same for most people. Anyway, because of the wet and the cold I got chilblains on my hands and feet and it was so bad they bled, so I had to give up and go home. I had to go home in Mr Dale's slippers, a little tich like me in size tens.

Mrs Dale's daughter Mary was a lovely little girl, she was very fond of me and I loved her. She couldn't talk very well and would say, "I'm going to stir the eliza wiv Gwadys." She meant the steriliser. After I left, we kept friends and I visited and stayed a time or two. The last time that I stayed, she slept with me, with her arms tight around my neck. Some time later I had a message that she'd died of TB meningitis; she was only eight. It was tragic.

So I went into private service, working for Mr and Mrs Davis who lived at 17 Westwood Road in Leek, and later moved up to Buxton Road. Mr Davis was the manager of the Midland Bank in Derby Street. I was there for two or three years, then left to work in Tatton's Dyeworks at Upperhulme. Mrs Davis was cross that I was leaving.

I went to work with my sister Phyllis. We did five days and Saturday mornings. You had to be at work for eight o' clock, and if you were a minute late you were docked quarter of an hours pay. I did silk purning, where you took silk from a bobbin and it went onto a purn. The purn fitted onto a spindle. I enjoyed the work, it was warm and dry and you had fun with the others. It was very friendly.

Phyllis was always a bit of a tomboy and one day she was busy talking, out of her place, instead of getting on with her work, when she saw Max Tatton coming along. So Bill Bratt pushed her into a box of yarn and dropped the lid. Well Max Tatton must have seen something and came and lifted the lid, Phyllis had to crawl out, and he said to her, "Don't get in there, you'll spoil the yarn." She would have been sacked if the war hadn't been on. Tatton's were alright to work for, mother used to say they found people work, there wouldn't have been much without them. They were very busy at one time, they ran a bus in from Longnor way.

We lodged in the week with Colin and Annie Lowndes at Broncott, just five minutes away from the works. They were very easy going and homely, we had our dinner there. One night, we came in late, they always left the door loose, and we had a shock. There were two Americans asleep on the sofa.

We walked past the chapel and when old Mr Parker from near the bridge died, they laid him out in the chapel for several days - there wasn't enough room in the house. So every time we walked past, Phyllis thought she saw his face at the window. It was only in her imagination.

Cycling from Hocker to work one Monday morning in winter, the roads were dreadful icy and it would hardly be light. The bikes went from under us and went skidding off down the road on their own. And I remember there were four men painting windows at the works once. They were four storeys up, on

Mabel Belfield and Gladys Finney.

scaffolding, when something broke. Two of them fell into the brook and were badly hurt.

In wartime, we did silk for parachutes. There were air raid precautions, where we put our tin hats on and went to the shelter, dug out below Day's farm. I remember on my twenty-first birthday, we walked over to see the crashed German bomber near Goldsitch Moss. It had been coming back from bombing Liverpool. We saw the bodies, but we weren't shocked; just glad that it was one less German plane. What a way to celebrate your twenty-first birthday.

My brother Edwin worked at New Grange, Meerbrook for Mr Hine. The War Ag sent a letter for him and the roads were blocked with snow, so Phyllis and I walked all the way from the Hocker to take it for him. But Mr Hine told them that if they took Ted, he wouldn't plough a furrow, so Ted never went; none of my brothers went, they were all doing farm work. It was a worry less for my mother.

A couple of years into the war, the War Office asked each factory to supply so many of its workers to go into munitions manufacture. I was chosen to go along with four others; Freda and Doris Hine from Blackshaw Moor, and Mary and Florrie Belfield from Five Clouds. We were sent to Leicester, where we were trained to use a capstan lathe. Then you had to take an exam. I think Mary and Florrie failed theirs and went home. We worked nights, twelve hour shifts. You stood at the lathe all night with lubricant like milk running down - we made parts for Lancaster Bombers. I once lost a finger end.

It was a big place and the pay was good, I think my first pay was £5 and so many shillings - I do know it was stolen. I enjoyed it there; I made some good friends who I kept in contact with. We were at Leicester for three months, then they moved us to Burton and we were there for three years. We tried to come home weekends if we could, by bus or train. Going back to work was by train from Leek to Uttoxeter, then to Tutbury, we liked to catch Tutbury Ginnie, a little train that ran between Burton and Tutbury. And I had good digs with Mrs Stone in Victoria Street.

After the war I got married in 1946, and went to live at Longsdon. In the 1947 winter, I walked from there to the Hocker to see if Mum and Dad were alright. I stayed the night, then walked back the next day stopping to see

Mr Phillips, Oakenclough.

friends at Upperhulme on the way. And it was while I was there that news came through that a plane had crashed on Grindon Moor trying to get supplies through to stranded villages.

When we had children of our own, I took them to Rudyard chapel. They had a choir there and old Mr Buxton conducted them. I well remember one time a little voice saying, "Are those naughty ladies 'cause man's got a stick to them." It was my Julie.

New Grange, Meerbrook. The farm on the left was Hine's, that on the right was Robinson's. The farms were demolished for the new reservoir and all the foreground is now flooded.

Vic Rider

I was born in 1918, the youngest of six children. There was Jessie, Katy and Alice; Mary and Harry died aged about two and three, I think from something like pneumonia. Mum was a Ferns from Onecote before she was married.

Dad was a blacksmith, here at Carriage House. They made their own shoes then, he had a helper, a striker, Harold Phillips. And my uncle Dick Rider helped for a while. He had a blacksmith's shop at the back of the Three Horseshoes in Meerbrook and ended up in Russell Street in Leek.

I've seen as many as twelve horses waiting in this yard to be shod, and some would have to go home and come back another day because he couldn't do them all in the day. It was mostly heavy farm horses then. A set of new shoes put on, in the early thirties, cost 7s 6d. If the shoes were taken off, the feet pared and the shoes put back on, that was called four removes and cost 4s. But there wasn't much left by the time the striker was paid.

Dad wouldn't let me be a blacksmith, he said it was too heavy a job mauling under horses. He got cancer in his leg, and wondered if it had started from a kick. He had his leg taken off and when he got over that, he had an artificial leg and made chain harrows for farmers. He forged them himself and made a pattern thing to bend the metal round. I helped to sharpen the spikes and put a thread on and build them up. He worked for twelve months, then the cancer came back on his lungs. He died in 1940, aged sixty.

Outside the Upperhulme shop in the late 1920s.
Vic Rider. Mary Tatton and Norman Blades behind.

Mum kept the Smithy going for a while - a man came from Leek on Tatton's bus - but after paying him there wasn't much left, and with tractors coming in and less horses she packed it up.

Mr Agar kept the post office. It was up the road above the New Inn, which is now the Rock Inn. His son Ronnie was my mate. We went chapel Sunday School, and later were in Meerbrook church choir when we were older, along with Dick Lownds. Ronnie was killed in France in the war.

Mr Parker looked after the chapel, and when he died, his grandson Maurice did it. Jimmy Bloor, from Corner House took the Sunday School for a good while.

The postman, Mr Spencer, walked from Leek to Meerbrook, left their letters, then walked up Whitty Lane, or through the fields, dished the letters out round here, then took up to our post office - Billy Mellor did from there and higher up. Then he stopped in a little stone shed by the Homestead cobbling all day, mending boots and shoes. At night, he'd pick up the letters from our post office, then on to Meerbrook post office to pick theirs up, then walk back to Leek. That was for a good while before the war. Eh, when you think what they did in them days, in all weathers, and only Sunday off.

Before the war, on summer nights, we used to play cricket or football at the back of Buttyfold. Eric Goldstraw, Pat McCarthy, Ronnie Agar, Charlie Clowes, Dick Lownds, any local lads. You had to make your own entertainment. But the war broke a lot of things up.

I started work aged fourteen at Tatton's Mill across the road. I got 10s a week, and then with a few coppers taken out for hospital and the like, I was left with 9s, for 48hrs. I worked there for forty years, till it was shut down in 1970 when we were made redundant. There was Upperhulme, Buxton Road, Golbourne and Mayfield. They were taken over and they're all gone now, except Mayfield, that's Mayfield Yarns now.

I was works' engineer when I finished, keeping machines going. I had fourteen men under me, joiners, bricklayers, electricians, stokers. At first, they had a big tubular boiler, then that was taken out and there was a new boilerhouse with two coal-fired Lancashire boilers. George Collier and Eric Clowes worked on them.

I enjoyed my work fairly well, but there was a lot of worry. I was under Isaac Birch when I started, he was manager of the winding department. Mr Brookes was manager of the dyehouse. Wilfred Brookes took over matching colours, Horace Leech was another. It was hand dyeing, skein dyeing then days. They made a good artificial black; the water must have suited. It was filtered with two filters and there were two softening plants. Then it was stored in tanks for the dyehouse.

There were two fire engines, you could have towed them but they were used as pumps. There was water underneath, and all you needed to do was drop your suction pipes in and couple the hoses up. There was a fire main all round the mill, with reels at various points. It was well protected. I suppose that was after the warping room burnt down.

I'd be 16 or 17 then and Simpson's cotton mill at Mayfield was empty, so Max Tatton bought it and the workers from the warping room were bussed over there. I went for a time. In the warping room there were creels with several hundred bobbins on, and layers of yarn were put onto a beam or warp. The weft room was at this end; in there they put purns onto a shuttle for weaving. Some of the yarn was sized after being warped, it was put through size to stiffen it, then went onto steam-heated drums to dry it.

In the war there was the air-raid shelter across the road. They had a generator for lights and there was a safe where the books were locked in every night in case the mill was bombed and burnt.

When the Yanks went from the camp on Blackshaw Moor, the Poles came and some of them worked in the quarries at Buxton; there was a bus to take them. I drove a bus for Tatton's for a good while, each end of the day. Eh, we had some rough journeys in winter on the Longnor and Newtown run. Billy Ball drove another bus, picking up from round Warslow and Butterton. I used to leave my bus at night at Gee's garage at New Road - that's between Longnor and Warslow - and come back with him, it saved running two buses back. Then in a morning, he'd bring some men in for quarter to seven and pick me up - we

Ramshaw School
Back: Ray Trafford (teacher), Jimmy Mountfort, Vic Rider, Mo Grindey, Ronnie Ager, Dick Lowndes, – –, Ray Clowes, Josie Ager
3rd Row: Annie Mountfort, – – Whittaker, Ray Grindey, Jack Brunt, – – Whittaker, Fred Brunt, – – Byatt, Wilf Mycock, Harry Gibson, Annie Downes
2nd Row: – – Brunt, Phyllis Grindey, May Clowes, Gladys Mycock, – – Mycock, – –, – –, – –, – –, – – Trafford, Edie Lowndes
Front: – –, Eric Clowes, Ralph Dale, – –, Reg Brunt, – –, – –, Stuart Wilde, Maurice Parker

met at the chapel. Then we picked my bus up, and he went off on his run. I picked up from Newtown and Longnor, Bradburys from Barrow Moor, and Jimmy Bloor, Eric Bratt, Herbert Wilde, Annie Potter and Stanley Wheeldon from Middle Hills. It was a struggle some nights in bad weather to get back; we had to go round by Bottom House. In 1947, we never went for five weeks, the roads were level full of snow; there was no tackle in them days to clear it like now. And they wouldn't be paid then if they couldn't get. I suppose those who could get would have to do overtime.

I've spent some hours watching the water wheel going round at Dain's Mill. I remember seeing Mr Hine grinding hen beans into split corn. The corn came from Macclesfield on steam wagons. They were Sentinels and had pneumatic tyres, not solid ones. Tattons had a steam wagon. They took parcels to Leek Station and fetched coal back. That would be late twenties. Mr Sam Beswick from Ferny Knowle fetched from Leek station with horses before that. The wagon was a Burrell, earlier than a Sentinel. If they weren't busy, they'd use it to fetch lime from Buxton for farmers.

Sammy Wood was a driver and coming down Cat Tor one day, he was braking on his fly wheel and it burst, a piece hit him on the head and killed him. There were two men on the wagon, a driver and a fireman. The other man, Walter Heath managed to turn it into the side and stop it. I remember him coming down like mad, sweating and cap in hand, to tell Max Tatton. He had a Daimler and he jumped in and backed up the road to take Sammy to hospital - there was nowhere to turn. It was a very bendy road as well as being steep before it was straightened. There were a lot of accidents with lorries fetching lime and stone; their brakes would go and they couldn't get round the corners.

Vic and Philip Rider.

Hilda Scott and Mary Rider in Tatton's office.

Vic and John Rider.

Blackshaw Moor.

The Tatton's coach stuck in snow.

Below: Charlie Day, Hilda, Mr Wheelton and Alec Day. Delivering the milk in 1947.

A sledge outside Abbey Farm about 1900.

Blackshaw Moor camp in 1963.

Charlie and Jessie Day's wedding in 1923 at Upperhulme.

Jean Hulme & Edna Goldstraw

Our Day forefathers were at Cheddleton. We have records of them being at Paper Mill House, and doing work on the wheel at the flint mill. They had coaches and horses for hire, a coal business and a milk round. When they came to Edge End, Leek, it was a big milk round, which was later split into three between Dad, Uncle Archie and Uncle Ron. After six generations it's still in the family with Edna's son Brian Barlow and his wife Glenys.

Dad and his two brothers went away in the first war. Dad was gone the longest; he went to the Middle East. He said it wasn't as bad as France; it was an experience, although there were some nasty jobs. He liked the Turks.

Mum lived at the Smithy at Carriage House, Upperhulme. On a Saturday morning she cycled to Leek to visit her Granny at Ball Haye Green. Dad used to see her going past Edge End, and one day he plucked up courage to ask her out. Eventually they got married and moved to Mile End on Blackshaw Moor. Mum's cousin, Charlie Clowes, whose mother had died in childbirth, went to live with them and help. He was seventeen and for the first two years he had no wage, they couldn't afford to pay him. He ended up living with our family for the rest of his life. He was a very good cowman.

When they moved to Buttyfold Farm, Mum had a bit of help in the house. She had six children in nine years and helped with the milk round. Harry Ferns also came to live with us from Barnados. He was twelve when he came. Harry and Charlie were always like older brothers to us, and we never heard our parents ever have a wrong word with them.

Dad and Hilda did the milk round until Hilda got married, then we did it. We used a van taking bottles, and churns and a measure. So whatever vessel people brought to us we filled. The Polish people brought big bowls. Milk was rationed in the war, but people always had more than their ration. The Polish people became friends, we learnt some Polish, we knew everybody. Mum and Hilda did the round for a while in the war, and picked up school dinners in Leek to bring back to Meerbrook school. They used a little Austin Seven van and the Americans poked fun at it. They would pick the back end up and say they could carry it away.

We were on Blackshaw camp for 8am; there were some drops in Leek, Shirburn Road, East Street and Upperhulme. The camp was the biggest customer; soldiers on Anzio Camp 4. would have four, ten-gallon churns and we'd sometimes fetch more. There were four cookhouses, they had lots of bottles too as people came and went. And we took about twenty-seven gallons into Leek and ten gallons into Upperhulme. After the war the camp carried on for training and National Service. There were some Italian prisoners of war for a while and the Polish people had camps 1, 2 and 3. We were scared of the soldiers sometimes, Mum had drilled it into us to be careful, so we didn't go out on our own. The black Americans frightened us, we weren't used to them; yet some who visited us were nice. Aunty Katy and Uncle Ernie had lots of American visitors. People seemed glad they were here.

When the Polish people first came, Dad brought a girl back one day. She had no mother and couldn't speak a word of English. Dad said "Do something with her." So we had a walk up Roche Road, then she helped do tea. I got her to butter some bread, she

Edna Day and Rhona Brooks   Buttyfold.

Charlie Day.

pulled it into lumps first, we weren't used to that either. They were very nice people, we got to know them well and saw them have children and grow up. There were some tragic stories. One day a lady was crying and swinging a key on a piece of string. When we asked what was the matter, she said "This is my key, all I've got left of my home. I locked my door and brought the key with me. Today would have been my daughter's birthday. When I asked for some milk for her, she was one year old, a soldier took her from me and I never saw her again."

Another said they were so hungry, they'd dug up a dead horse to eat. One lady told us of the time she'd taken her daughter back to Poland to visit her family. She'd never felt at home here, but after a while the child said, "Can we go home," and then she felt England was home.

We did the round for thirty-seven years, a long time. It changed from churns and bottling on the farm to all bottles and buying the milk from Clover Dairies. In bad weather it was a struggle, you could get stuck and have to dig yourself out. There were some bad times through Solomons Hollow.

On a Friday at Buttyfold, everyone who came had a drop of whisky in their tea and a cream cake. One day through the window we saw the vicar, Mr Walmsley, coming up the yard. Mum said, "Hide that whisky bottle quick, he'll think we've been drinking." When he came in we said, "You're just in time for Holy Communion." And after that every Friday was known as Holy Communion day.

Jack Hulme

Young Farmers at Leek Show. The first show after the War with the Earl of Shrewsbury and his wife.
Stan Hulme 3rd from left.

Jack Hulme.

Oil rig on Gun Hill late 1930s.

Jean Hulme

I met my husband Stan at a Meerbrook dance. He came from Horsecroft, down over Stoney Bridge over the River Churnet and through Hillswood.

His father Jack Hulme farmed Horsecroft, it was about seventy acres then, and with his brother they farmed Haregate Hall land, which they rented from Mr Argles. They kept dairy cows and did a milk round in Leek. He lost his first wife, which left him with two little children, Flo, aged two and Jack aged 9 months. Jack was reared with Bill Hulme's family and Granny Hulme reared Flo at home. He remarried when Flo was twelve and Jack went home when he started work at fourteen. Then there were three more children, Peggy, Alma and Stan.

Jack senior was always known as Gentleman John, because he was always immaculately dressed. When he sold milk, he always wore a spotless white slop (jacket) and polished brown leggings and a tie. He loved his horses and kept them in use long after his neighbours had tractors. He liked a drink on a Wednesday, and sometimes had too much! One day he came walking up Ball Haye Green with five horses that he'd bought in the market, manes tied to tails. The next week he had to sell them all.

Jack and his brother Harry used to fight a lot. Both did a milk round and locals remember that if they met at the top of Ball Haye Green, they'd get their horsewhips out and whip each other's horse. The milk was in churns and sometimes if the driver was with a customer they'd still whip the horse as they passed, causing it to bolt off spilling the milk everywhere.

Stan's mum got up every morning at 3am and Stan and his father at 5am. Everything was done exactly to time. They finished at night at 7pm and worked all day Saturday. The only time they had off was on Sunday from 12.30 till 4pm. I never knew what it was like to cook for Stan because he had all his meals at home and I was at Buttyfold. Even on a Sunday, it was a quick lunch, then get the children to Upperhulme Sunday school, then back to Horsecroft for 4 o'clock. But there were never any grumbles from anybody, the time we had together was precious.

All the hedges and ditches were done by hand; Stan did the hedges right up till his Dad died in the early 1970s.

Jack with his children and grandchild, 1930s.

At Haregate Hall.
Martin and Charles Argles
with Alma Hulme.

Right to left: Jack Hulme,
Charlie Hulme, Jack Hulme
Jnr, Stan Hulme. 1930s.

Flo and Stan at
Horsecroft.

May Day celebrations at Haregate ?1920s.

Left: Stan and his mother.

Below: Haregate Hall drawn in 1890 by Mackaness.

Visit of H.R.H. Princess Mary, of Cambridge, with Prince Teck.

TO THE "ROCHES" SWYTHAMLEY, AUGUST 23RD, 1872.

The 'Queen's Chair', carved out of the rockface for the Royal visit, can still be seen above Rock Hall.

MEERBROOK is a small village and hamlet of the township of Leek Frith, in the parish of Leek, 10 miles south-east of Macclesfield, 9 south-west of Longnor, and 4 north of Leek station, its post town; it is in Totmonslow hundred, Leek county court district, Lichfield diocese, Stafford archdeaconry, and Leek deanery, North Staffordshire. The living is a curacy, possessing 84½ acres of glebe land and residence; the presentation is claimed by the vicar of Leek and also by the inhabitants; the Rev. James Turner is the incumbent. The church of St. Matthew is a small ancient edifice, built nearly 300 years ago by Sir Ralph Bagnall, and has a tower with 1 bell. The interior is very neat, with open pews. The Free school is endowed with bequests producing £12 5s. yearly. The village is pleasantly situate about half-a-mile from a range of huge tremendous cliffs, called "The Roches," which are composed of large heaps of rude and rugged rock piled one upon another, and have a most terrific and singularly irregular appearance. They are of sandy grit formation. From the falling of portions of the rock at various times, a very curious habitation has been formed, in which a family now reside; the roof consists of an immense stone which covers space sufficient for two good-sized rooms; it is designated Rock Hall. There is also another remarkable cavern called Lud Church, well worthy of notice. The population is included in that of the township of Leek Frith. The Earl of Macclesfield is lord of the manor. There are annual charities amounting to 30s. distributed in bread; 17s. to the poor of Roachside and Haslewood; £2 to the poor of Gunside; a gift of £2 10s. in bibles, and £4 in clothing. James Mabberly, late clerk to Meerbrook church, bequeathed three small cottages and one acre of land, now producing £10 per annum, given in bread to the poor attending Meerbrook church.

PRIVATE RESIDENTS.
Hine Mr. Joseph
Turner Rev. James, M.A

COMMERCIAL.
Arnett Charles, *Fountain*
Bayley Edwd. farmer, North hill woods
Belfield George, farmer, Old springs
Bellfield Joseph, farmer, Clough head
Billinge William, farmer, New grange
Bratt Joseph, shoemaker
Brown John, farmer, High forest
Brown Matthew, farmer, Westwood
Brown Thos. farmer, Pheasant's clough
Free School, Samuel Beresford, master

Carter Thomas, farmer, Gunside
Chapel Joseph, farmer, New house
Clulow James & John, farmers, Alderlee
Clulow John, farmer, Meadow
Cooper Moses, farmer, Stock meadow
Dakin Charles, farmer, Thorney lee
Fisher Robert, stonemason
Hine George, farmer, Roach grange
Hine James, farmer, Oxhay
Hine Joseph, jun. farmer, Green lane
Hine William, farmer, Old lodge
Hine William, farmer, New set
Lomas William, farmer, Roach grange
Mumfort Richard, *Three Horse Shoes*

Mountfort Samuel, farmer, Windy gates
Nixon Robert, farmer & parish clerk, New Bees
Reed Joseph, farmer, Thorney lee
Rider George, wheelwright
Rider Thomas, blacksmith
Simpson John, shopkeeper
Taylor Thomas, farmer, Park house
Taylor William, farmer, Brown set
Wheeldon John, shoemaker
Wood Richard, farmer
Wood William, shoemaker
Letters received through Leek by foot post

The Meerbrook entry in Kelly's Directory for 1860 shows many familiar local names of today.

Joe Day

I was born in 1929 at Buttyfold Farm, Upperhulme. Mum and Dad had only come there the year before. They rented it from the Church but some years later they were able to buy it. Mr Carter had farmed it before, and when Dad went to look at the farm he told him, "You'll do no good here." He had lost a lot of cows with Johnes disease. Dad thought it was because the drinking places of the cows were polluted. So he decided to take the farm, and the first thing he did was to put a hydraulic ram in the brook down at Dain's Mill, and pump fresh water up. It seemed to do the trick because they went on alright.

They kept dairy cows, pigs and a lot of hens. They had a milk round and sold some of the milk on that, the rest would go to Manchester. Mum sometimes did the milk round then; she had to be at the Workhouse in Ashbourne Road at seven-thirty in the morning. One day some harness broke, and the horse bolted across Blackshaw Moor. Luckily Arthur Clowes, who worked at Benisons at Tittesworth, managed to stop it.

I went to Thorncliffe school when I was five; it's a long walk for a little lad all the way across Blackshaw Moor and up Thorncliffe Lane. On that first day, my brother Alec and Harold Pickford took me, then at night they ran back and left me. But I ran after them and stopped at Granny Ryder's at the smithy. She nearly murdered them because I was in a right state. Later on, one time, I remember the teacher, Mrs Scott, sending a couple of us to Ramshaw school with a message, and we got lost going through the fields.

I suppose the biggest effect on my young life was the war. There were quite a lot of plane crashes round here. There was a Lancaster crashed on the back of the Roches; I think it was on a Wednesday in a snowstorm; they'd perhaps be lost. Jess Tunnicliffe saw it go over Blue Hills. Us lads went up on the Sunday, there'd perhaps be seven of us, Alec, Harold Pickford, John Day and some others. It didn't seem as if anyone had been near. Through a door I could see a fur lined boot and I put my hand in to get it, I couldn't see any further. But it seemed to be fast, I think the man's foot might have still been in it and I left it alone.

We found two bombs, one red and one khaki, about two feet long with fins on. We carried them up to the rocks above Rockhall: our idea was to throw them over the edge and see if they went off. When we got near the Queens Chair, we were trying to get them over a wall and Alec got worried that if we dropped them accidentally, they'd blow up. So he persuaded us to leave them under the wall. We didn't take much convincing, they were heavy and it was rough going.

Then there were two Seafires - naval planes - crashed further over. We went up one night on motorbikes to have a look. They'd crashed side by side.

Charlie Clowes and Alec were in the Home Guard. A German Junkers 88 bomber went down at Quarnford, so Alec and I walked up the next night. Jimmy Fisher was there, he'd been with Max Tatton to Liverpool - they were on Defence. He said the devastation from the bombing was dreadful, a butter and margarine factory had been hit and on fire, and the stuff was running down the street up to your knees. He was pleased the plane had been shot down. The bodies of five Germans lay side by side, they'd been moved together but not taken away at that time. They were badly burnt, to me they looked like cooked sausages. I'll never forget it, some things stick in your mind don't they? I think they were buried in Leek Cemetery.

Another day I was at Uncle Archie's farm on Blackshaw Moor, when we heard a funny "woof" down the chimney. We thought a plane had gone over but it was a Spitfire crashing near Far House. It came through the Roches from Quarnford and went down near to Jacky Brough's house. It went into the ground that far they never got it out till about twenty years ago, when they got the engine out.

Then there was a Wellington went down on the side of Hen Cloud. My sister Hilda had just come back from milk selling, and she was in Uncle Vic's yard at the smithy. She saw it come over twisting and trying to turn; it took the top of one of our walls out and some fir trees as it crashed. Alec and Mr Wheelton were first there, the plane was on fire and they said rounds of bullets were hanging from trees and going off with the heat. It was very dangerous. Only one man survived, the rear gunner, an Australian. He came back about ten years ago to have another look.

An American 'Thunderbolt' crashed on our land at Thorncliffe. A hundred yards away on the road, the local bobby found a man's hand. He thought the pilot might have pushed his cockpit open to bail out, and it had slammed shut on him and cut it off.

Hilda was a friend of Smiths in Leek, whose son Keith was a navigator. Flying over Leek one day he dropped his socks out and they landed in Ashbourne Road. It was said the bobbies got them and he told them to keep them, they needed washing. Anyway Hilda came from Leek one Wednesday and said Keith was missing. He'd gone on a bombing trip, volunteering for a mate who wasn't very well. That same day, I'd been grinding corn with the mill and lost the end of a finger. And a Lightning crashed above the Strines.

Later in the war, Charlie and I were bringing a load of hay out of Blackshaw meadows and there was a plane circling. Charlie was driving and I was riding behind. He says, "Where's that plane gone?" He'd landed in the field and was taxiing up behind us. And within three days we'd had both fields taken off us. There were five planes and forty-gallon oil drums at the top end, it was like a little airfield. They were Lysander spotter planes for the American big guns. One day a bad wind blew up and one plane couldn't land, and ended up part crashing above the road in uncle Archie's field; so they decided to move.   I think they went Ashbourne way. The main road may have put them off for safety reasons.

One time we were in a plough field and five British planes came over, then a twin engine Dakota came past low. I'd climbed onto a stone gatepost, and I reckon it was nearly level with me. It was a transport plane, and the door was open. I could see a man on a swivel chair, and he turned round as he passed and waved at me. There was a hencote, they must have only been feet off it. You wouldn't believe how low they could go. They had to practice low flying for special manouvres to avoid radar and anti-aircraft stuff.

Another time I remember, Manchester was being bombed and some of us had walked up Roche Road with Mum to see if we could see anything. Looking that way the sky seemed alight. Suddenly a bomb dropped close by, Mum ducked down and cut her knee. It was actually quite a few fields away, down on Whitty Lane, close to Middle Hulme, but it seemed very close. It was said after, that a farmer down there had shown a light and a plane going back from Manchester had jettisoned a bomb, but I don't know if that's true.

The Americans built the army camp on Blackshaw Moor; they bussed labourers in from the Potteries. It became a very busy place; they had everything, to us they lived like kings. We fetched swill from the camp for the pigs, but there was that much stuff you couldn't use it all. There'd be a ten-gallon bin full of dough, coming over the top till you couldn't see the bin. Or a bin full of apricots.

We had a barn down the fields, we called it Ballhay barn, and about ten women took up residence in it -I think they came from Liverpool - and soldiers would visit them. The local bobby daren't go down after being told they'd cut his throat if he interfered. He said, "They can do what they want, I'm not going down again." One Sunday, us lads went down and threw a firework. It landed by the door but didn't go off, so one of us crept down and relit it. Well it went off quick, and two big black men came out and ran after us; we only just managed to get away. Another time we sneaked down and Alec was peeping through the keyhole. He says, "I can't see anything." Then he realised there was a man peeping back from the other side.

We grew some corn down there, and there was a hen cote that we put hens in to clear spilt grain up after harvest. The soldiers and women were using this too, and we knew. Alec and I were fencing down there one day, and we saw the cote was fastened on the outside, so we thought "There'll be no-one in, we'll have a look." What we didn't know was there had been some one down and fastened two Yanks and two women in. So when we opened the door, we had a shock. Alec said "Hello," and shut the door again.

At night, Blackshaw Moor was heaving with women from Leek and beyond, Uncle Vic counted over a hundred one night as he was going to Leek. And some would have husbands away fighting, but you could hardly blame them, the Yanks had everything they wanted.

Some of them were grand folks, they'd come and help us when they had time off. One day we were carting corn in Blackshaw meadow. Geoff Brooks was a young lad, and he was climbing up the front of the trailer when he missed his footing and fell, landing heavily on the trailer draw bar. An American officer was helping us, and he picked him up and said to my Dad, "These young 'uns will bounce, he'll be alright, he's had a lucky escape." My Dad trusted him. And there was a Polish officer who came and helped. He was a blacksmith, a big strong fellow, seventeen or eighteen stone. He'd been hedgelaying with us one day, and he ran down the field and somersaulted right over landing on his feet. He could do it like drinking tea, he was that fit.

Mr Wheelton, Joe and Charlie Clowes.

Before the Normandy invasion, several of Uncle Archie's fields up Thorncliffe Lane were taken, and filled with heavy tackle and half-tracked vehicles. Then one night they came off in wet weather, and next morning there was that much mud and gravel on the roads you couldn't get across them in a car. They had to get a bulldozer and clear it up. Everything was gone, hundreds of army tents, all gone.

Dad had been in the first war, in the Middle East as a transport driver. He often spoke about Baghdad, Mesopotamia and the River Tigris. One day in the desert a plane came and dropped a row of bombs; one landed in front of him and one behind. Another time a plane came bombing and the guns couldn't reach him, so they towed one up a hill to get extra range, and next time they got him. Once they'd a train of camels with them and they lay down and wouldn't move. The Arabs said "There's a sandstorm coming and the camels know." The storm came, they just shut their eyes and nostrils and the sand blew over them. When it had finished, they stood up, shook themselves and set off. But not one wagon would start, they were all full of sand. Another time they were in a quarry and the officer said, "We're not stopping here any longer." Shortly afterwards it was bombed. Dad always said, you were lucky if you got away.

Later on after the war we decided to get a small lorry. Uncle Ernie worked at Rainow at Frankie Jackson's yard. He ran about twenty wagons carting churns or anything. Uncle Ernie said, "There's a good wagon coming off the road that'll just suit you." So I went to fetch it, I'd never driven a wagon before, and uncle Ernie was going to come back with me. You could drive one on a car license then, and after so many years they gave you your HGV. Well, the phone went, and uncle says, "That's buggered it Joe, there's a wagon broke down, and I've got to go out to it. You'll have to wait three hours or take it back yourself. I think you'll get back alright, just remember those back wheels are coming behind you; don't turn corners quick, or they could go over the top of somebody."

I was no age, I can remember coming through Macclesfield as if it were yesterday. The first time I ever drove a wagon! I got back alright. We had several wagons after that. We had a lot of work put to us as we didn't really want, carting stuff about, I don't know how we found the time. Uncle Percy got us orders for sugar beet pulp. So we put tall sides on. It was a seven ton wagon but we got twelve tons on, they didn't bother then. We picked the pulp up from perhaps five stations then, Leek, Cheddleton, Bradnop. There were seventeen tons of wet pulp on a train truck, and you had to shovel it all out by hand onto your wagon, take it and shovel it off, then come back for the rest. It was very hard work and I was usually on my own, though sometimes Reg or Alec went instead. You couldn't be too long unloading, because you had to pay 'demuridge' if the truck was held for more than two days.

One day someone had been throwing a load off rough and had spilt pulp everywhere. I was trying to draw my wagon away, and skidded into the truck and got stuck. They were shunting and only just spotted me in time. We had to get some railway sleepers and just get it moved enough for them to shunt. Once I had Mick Lomas helping me, he was only a school lad. I wasn't very well, I was starting shingles. We were carting sugar beet to Gooseneck Farm, and the old man wouldn't let the farm lad help to unload. So with all the sweating I caught a chill as well, I was very poorly, and I've got the scars on my back to this day.

Meerbrook School Sports late 1950s.

Back row: Brenda Robinson, Freda Robinson, Barbara Ferns, Roy Goldstraw, Jim Robinson, Philip Riley, Brian Rider, Norman Hill, Shirley Allen, Geoff Robinson, Carol Ferns, Graham Cooper.

Middle row: Barbara Robinson, Jackie Torr, Sidney Bowers, Pete Goldstraw, Derek Wooliscroft, Joyce Robinson, Marilyn Wooliscroft, Derek Robinson, Michael Fernihough, Graham Robinson.

Front row: Ian Dugmore, Pat Bowers, Pamela Clulow, Geoff Allen (?), Martin Hyde, Cath Ferns, Linda Fernihough, -- Dickinson (?), Graham Goldstraw.

Upperhulme early 20th century.

Buttyfold

Mary Pickford

When I was a child, we lived at Thorn Bank Farm, Bottomhouse. My Dad was William Salt, a fairly big farmer in those days. But he was taken poorly and his family must have known it was terminal, because they visited him and persuaded him to leave the farm to them. So when he died, my Mum, Clara, had nothing but a small annual allowance for me; I was only six. Mum had to go out to work, she did housekeeping for a vicar at Ipstones and they couldn't do with a child, so I had to go to my Aunt's at Carriage House, Upperhulme to be reared.

When I left school I went to work at Tattons. I did coning or packing or scarf work, where the material came in for dyeing and steaming, pressed into big lengths, ready to go back into Leek factories to be made up into scarves and hats. It was a good place to work, the wages were ordinary but it was close to, and you had a bit of fun; I enjoyed it.

I used to go to dances with Edna Day, we were the same age. Sometimes we walked over to Swythamley; that was a nice place, perhaps half a dozen times a year. We went with our dinky curlers in, and took them out when we got there. And we went to dances at Ramshaw school. That would be Friday night. Then there might be a dance at Meerbrook on Saturday night. We had to ask Mum for permission to go to both. We walked all the way round by the road, I remember my shoes would be hurting going back; but if there were boys with us you forgot it. I met my husband Harold when we were fourteen and fifteen. He lived and worked in Upperhulme. We spent a lot of time together off and on until we got married.

When Mum got older she wanted a cottage of her own; she'd been living at Buttyfold for a while with my cousin Jessie. So Mr Grove, the vicar at Meerbrook, said she could have one of the Church cottages. Well, when it came to going she decided she didn't want to go, she'd never lived on her own. So she gave it up; but as soon as she gave it up she wanted it back. Mr Grove was very good and he let her have the next one. So she had the middle one, between Mrs Deaville and Mrs Bratt from Wetwood. She was a big churchgoer, and always put her collection on the mantlepiece ready even if she couldn't go. The water had to be fetched from the pump across the road, but when Mr Walmsley was vicar he went down and fetched them coal and water in. Those cottages were grand for the old people then, they were small but sufficient, she loved it there.

Eleanor and Gwen Thompson, who worked at Tattons, outside the New Inn at Upperhulme.

More girls who worked at Tattons. Anne Wilkinson, Nellie Weston and Jean Grindey.

Swythamley School at Gun End, 1924.

Olive Wilshaw

I was born in 1927 at Turner's Pool Farm, Swythamley. My parents and grandparents were tenants on the Swythamley estate. My grandparents took the farm in 1854.

In times past the old road over Gun used to come down through Old Hag and Turner's Pool. Old Hag was a pub, and there was a schoolroom added to our house, with a bedroom over for the teacher. We still have some old school books from the 1700s. I wonder who would spend the money to make the school - maybe the Traffords, who owned Swythamley estate then?

The road would then go on to Swythamley and Wincle Grange. It was said the monks from Dieulacres Abbey used it to travel between granges and to take wool to Chester. Maybe they would take fish from the pool back to the Abbey.

Mum used to work in Macclesfield, in a bakeshop, before she was married. This was around 1918. She used to talk about the flu epidemic. Customers would come into the shop, have a coffee and fall asleep, and afterwards they wouldn't be seen again. They'd died! It was awful but luckily she didn't get it. If she hadn't told us about it we wouldn't have known anything, it wasn't spoken of in the countryside.

We went to Gun End school. We had to walk a mile through the fields in clogs because the grass was usually wet, either with rain or dew. We would moan "Oh no, not these again!" because the other children didn't wear them. We changed into something else at school. I remember my Dad buying my first pair of wellies.

I went to Gun End school until I was 11, then to Rushton for two years until Milner Hall was built in Leek. I went there for a year. We had a taxi to Rushton school, and a bus to Leek, both from Gun End.

At Gun End school we had one teacher for all the children, no matter what their age difference. And some passed their exams and went on to Westwood High School. The teacher would set different lessons for different age groups. Her name was Miss Condlyffe, and she lived in Rushton.

In the schoolroom there was a big fireguard around the stove, and the teacher would put coats on it to dry if they were wet. And a kettle on top to make cocoa. There was no free milk then, and no dinners at Gun End, we had to take sandwiches.

We'd be in the playground sometimes and see tramps going down the road towards Bearda. I don't know where they'd be going but I remember being frightened of them.

At Rushton school we could have a hot "torpedo." It was like a cornish pasty, from Mrs Turnock's shop in Sugar Street, opposite the school. This was a shop cum bakehouse. They cost 2d.

Also at Rushton, Mr Banks the headteacher always told us not to get on the "Feeder" if it was frozen. Of course living at Turner's Pool we knew not to go on ice. Well, one day I remember it had been frozen for weeks, and we'd walked to the shop at the end of the marsh. As we walked back there were a lot of children on the Feeder having a jolly time sliding about in their dinner hour. We stood watching and when the school bell rang the children ran up the field and climbed over the wall into the playground, instead of going round by the Royal Oak and up Sugar Street. So we thought we'd cross the Feeder and

Grandad and Granny Whittaker.

follow thinking we'd be late otherwise. But on getting into school the teacher said "All those who crossed the Feeder, come to me for punishment!"

Jubilee 1935 or Coronation 1937, I don't recall which, we had a celebration at Rushton. I can't remember how we got there but Dad asked Doug Poyser if he'd bring us home. He was a bit special, he had a car. We got to Daniel's Well, where all the schoolchildren from Rushton were joined by the children from Gun End. We paraded down Macclesfield Road to the Hanging Gate, turned up to go past the Crown, then across the 'Bandage' to a service at the church. Then we walked back the other way past the Knot. Tea and sports were at the school and we were given a mug.

Mum used to take eggs in a basket to Macclesfield. It would hold sixteen dozen and eight. She would have another basket with dressed poultry in, which had been ordered. Dad would take her in the horse and trap to Wincle church, where she would catch a bus to Macclesfield. There she would sell the produce from door to door, walking round the streets to where it was ordered. Then she'd catch the bus back to Wincle and walk home carrying the weeks groceries.

They had a big bag of flour to make the bread, and oatmeal for oatcakes and porridge, probably off the cornman. Sugar came in hundredweights from Jack Ball's, Sheepmarket, in Leek. Dad fetched that with the horse and trap. Salt was bought in lumps about two foot long, at least six inches square, perhaps weighing fourteen pounds. It was wrapped in brown paper and purchased from the grocer. You'd slice it up and put it in a saltbox for kitchen use. You hung the saltbox on the wall. The salt was cut into squares for cheesemaking.

Up to 1937 Mum and Dad would make cheese. After that, when the Milk Board was formed, they sold the milk. They'd have about twenty cows. The cheese was made from the summer milk. Cheese made from winter milk was not wanted. It was called booze cheese (probably a corruption of boost or stall fed). The cheeses were forty pounds in weight, and we had a room upstairs called the cheese room, where the floor was covered in them. They were stored until April when Macclesfield wholesalers would come out and offer to buy them before the making of the next summers cheese.

Before they came, Mum would haul all the cheeses downstairs and take the old binding off and put new cloths on then take them all back up again. She always received a ha'penny a pound more for her cheeses than the other local farmers because she presented them better. Some of the neighbours would grumble because she got more, but neighbours were real neighbours in those days, we were all in the same boat and needed each others help to survive. Perhaps some of the other farmers in the area traded their cheeses in Leek.

In the winter, most of the cows were dried off, but you still needed some milk for the house, and there was always a calf or two about so some milking carried on.

I remember seeing the curd being put through the grinder before going into the mould, then into the press. Everytime you went past the press you gave it another little turn. The whey was fed to the pigs.

You bought your cheesecloth in big rolls and cut it yourself, and fastened it up with flour paste. The only other things you needed were salt and rennet.

The pool was mainly for duck shooting, but Sir Philip allowed a man to fish in it once a year. You'd think living by the pool we'd not be short of water, but the drinking water came from a spring into a tank up the fields, and in a dry time we could be short. That water was also needed to cool the milk, as it was running. The pool water was too warm in hot weather. During the winter of 1963 we had to cut a square in the ice with an axe every day in the same place to let the cows drink. Only one could drink at a time. The ice was 18 inches thick.

The rent was paid twice a year. You had to go up to the Tenants' Hall at Swythamley. It was due in March and September, but Sir Philip gave three months grace, so it was actually paid in June and December. So in June there was a garden party for the tenants, and in December a Christmas party. There was also a Christmas party for all the children on the estate, which I went along to. The Tenants' hall had animal heads around the walls, trophies from previous trips abroad, and for Christmas, a beautiful tree on the stage. We had our tea, then every child had a present with their name on. I always ended up with a book. And before you went home they let balloons go all over the room. The parties stopped when the war came, and there was only one more, a really smashing do for all the tenants, maybe in the late sixties.

Lady Brocklehurst was in the ATS during the war and she would come home on leave for about ten days and help in the gardens at the hall - perhaps digging up rhododendrons and clearing shrubs. After the war the Brocklehursts separated and Sir Philip remarried.

Turner's Pool farmhouse

On the estate you had to keep your farm tidy, your sheds tarred annually, windows and doors painted regularly. The estate provided you with paint, green, brown or white. You had to keep things maintained because it would be the estate's job to do any repairs.

We had to put some lime on the land to keep it sweet, and show our lime bills at rent day to show that we had done it.

You weren't allowed to plough without permission or cut trees down. If you wanted a tree for posts or fencing you had to go and ask Sir Philip, and he would go and look at it. If a tree blew down you had to tell him, and he might send his men to fetch the usable wood and you were left with the firewood. The Brocklehursts liked their trees, Sir Philip's father planted a lot of trees on the roadsides around the estate. Sir Philip would ride around the estate on his horse periodically, but he didn't need to check on people. They respected him and generally did as he liked them to. But if there was a fire on the moor, he'd be out in a flash.

Because the estate was well keepered, we didn't have much trouble with foxes, considering the amount of hens we kept. We shut them up every night. A coop of broodies up the side of the brook went missing one night and the coop was smashed up, but we thought that was badgers. They are on the crest of Swythamley, but you rarely saw them then.

In the 1950s we were on our own, bringing children up. Still on rationing, but as long as you could pay your way, that was everything. We'd nothing in those days, compared with today, but we were satisfied. I wonder if the children of today are as contented, with all the things they have now. We'd have about a dozen sheep, twenty dairy cows, some pigs and hens. Jack Wooley fetched our eggs in the large thirty dozen boxes. Every farm he went to he left any child a penny. It doesn't sound much, but saved, it added up.

For the Coronation celebrations in 1953, we walked through the fields and down the

Harry Clowes and Bill Wilshaw.

road to Meerbrook as a family. There was a service, sports and tea. I remember children falling out, "They don't belong our school." I don't remember if there was a dance, we had to come home for milking.

The summer of 1954 was dreadful. It seemed to rain every day. We had managed to get a bit of hay, so Bill helped neighbours at Thornyleigh. They'd work the hay all day, then it would rain on it at night. This was October. They didn't get it. At the same time, one of my sons, Ken was three years old, and I'd pull him up the fields in the pushchair to the far meadow, which was ploughed with potatoes in it. These needed lifting. So I tried to get them up. After we'd finished jobs in the yard I'd go and lift some, then eventually we'd go with the horse and cart and fetch a load. Everyone struggled that year, I don't know how some got through.

Mother used to say 1927 was a wet summer, when I was born. Dad mowed Little Meadow with a scythe at four o' clock in the morning. There came a thunderstorm and the crop was never seen again, it was washed down the brook. In October, mother's grandma came here to look after me so Mum could help Dad try and get some hay. Dad would buy some turnips to help get through. They would be pulped. Stockfeed potatoes too. We'd boil potatoes for the hens, and mix it with Arthur Warren's Oat Dust. My parents did it and we carried on. That was a helpful extra feed in the war when corn was short. A good thing to have then was a horse because you got extra rations for it.

A great character was Harry Clowes from Bottom House. In the 1950s he'd come and stay with us for perhaps three weeks, then move on somewhere else. He'd do all sorts of odd jobs. He was a bit deaf, smoked a pipe of twist and could tell lots of stories. He'd go to his daughters in Leek on a Wednesday for a clean shirt. He once walked to us from Leek when he was eighty four. He used to say, "A man could live on beer and bread and cheese." He was about ninety seven when he died.

Ralph Dale, First World War

Haymaking at Swainsmoor. Dad (Ralph, Snr), Philip, with two visitors and Myrtle on the right. 1950s.

Philip Dale

My Dale forbears settled at Flash in the 17th century. They were farmers and packhorse men, carrying salt out of Cheshire, cheese to Sheffield and cutlery back; and silk buttons from Leek and Macclesfield. They built Daffodil Farm on Morridge Top and while droving cattle from Wales brought Welsh daffodil bulbs back with them, which gave the farm its name.

In 1907 my grandparents moved to Oxbatch Farm, further across Morridge towards Onecote. Grandma Dale was a local preacher, unusual in those days. From there they attended Elkstones chapel. My Dad took the Sunday school and they had a whistle band going.

When Dad was twenty-one, he went into the army. He was a cavalryman, a good horseman. When they were training in Sussex, he told us that during their morning gallop the farmer's carthorses would jump out of their fields and join them. He had several horses shot from under him in the war. He didn't like to talk of his experiences on the Somme, it was too traumatic. He was badly injured and gassed, lying in a pool of gas for some

My Dale grandparents around 1918.

time, he was burnt, his top lip disfigured badly and he grew a moustache to hide it. He spent a long time in hospital recovering after the war; shrapnel was coming out of his body for years.

Before the war, he was an art student and was going to make art his career, he even

Haymaking at Little Swainsmoor.
Ralph Jnr on left, with Mum on the load, then cousin Ralph below and an Irish worker to the right.

taught it for a while. But with one lung almost useless from the gas, doctors advised to give that up, as living in a town with the smog would kill him. So he had to farm.

Wind power at Swainsmoor.

While the war was on, the family had moved down to the Millhouse at Gradbach, so he worked there when he got better. The silk mill was disused then, so they kept a lot of hens, deep litter style, a novelty then, and went in for winter egg production, selling eggs when they were scarce and dear. The horses were kept underneath, and one time they'd been treated with turpentine for some ailment, and the odours got into the eggs. They had a lot back, and had to re-imburse their customers. They weren't very pleased.

Mum was Florrie Bainbridge, from Lapwing Hall, Newtown. When she left school, she went to work for my grandparents at Gradbach, and ended up marrying Dad. There were sometimes paying guests staying and Dad might take them for a midnight trip to Ludchurch in Back Forest, to see if they could catch sight of the ghost of the lady in white - which they sometimes did - it was Mum with a sheet. She once wished she hadn't done it when one man got very upset.

There were often concerts at Gradbach chapel, and once Grandad thought he'd go in his working trousers, which had been mended with a big patch on the backside. He sat on the seat, which had been lately varnished for a couple of hours, and when he got up to go, he left the patch behind. It was very embarrassing, he had to try to cover up and make a quick exit.

In 1925 when Mum and Dad got married, my grandparents moved to Little Swainsmoor, but they found there was too much travelling between places, and they started having trouble with thieving at Gradbach, having hens and eggs stolen. So they packed up, and all lived at Swainsmoor, where my brother Ralph was born, then Amy, Myrtle and later me.

Dad was always a local preacher, he was gone most Sundays and depending where he

My Mum, Florence Dale, delivered the post for a while during the War and after. It was 14 miles on foot.

was planned to be, he might be gone early, leaving Mum to do the milking. We kept eighteen

Haymaking at Swainsmoor. My mother, my sister, Myrtle, and myself.

A carriage at Swythamley Hall at the turn of the 20th century.

or twenty milkers and the churns had to be taken down to Cat Tor with horse and cart or later an old van. Dad often walked to services, or he might get a bus from the Buxton Road to perhaps Wetley Rocks. Then someone might bring him back home. He'd often be planned at Danebridge, they'd think it wasn't far, but it would be a six or seven mile walk. The rest of us went to Upperhulme chapel. Sunday School was at two o'clock, followed by the service at two-thirty. Then there'd be an evening service too, at times like the harvest. There were about a dozen of us in Sunday school then. When old Mr Parker was young, about a hundred and twenty years ago, there are records of around a hundred in Sunday School.

Dad carved these likenesses of his parents in stone on the outside wall of the farmhouse.

Dad had always got a tale to tell. One was of a man going to Leek Market on a Wednesday. He'd be very drunk, and they'd load him onto his horse and trap, the horse would know its way home - and you'd hear him singing at the top of his voice the old Sankey hymn, "Yield not to temptation, for yielding is sin." When he was young, there were still mowing gangs with scythes. And he heard tell of one man, who when the horse mowers came in, threw his scythe over the wall saying, "I always knew it was a tit's job!"

Meerbrook village looking towards the Three Horseshoes, at the turn of the 20th century.
The school is on the left and the post office is on the right

Meerbrook School in the 1920s.

A shooting party at Troutsdale. Mill owners and beaters.

Margaret Wooliscroft

Grandad Mountfort was born at Wardle Barn Farm in the 1880s; the eldest of eight children. It was only a small farm, they kept ten or twelve cows and made butter and cream which they took into Leek to sell on the market. It was taken in baskets on the horse and cart. The horse was always called 'Kit', I never remember a horse of another name. They also kept pigs.

So when Grandad farmed on his own, with it only being a small place, he was the gamekeeper for Mr Argles of Haregate Hall, who owned all the land around. It was his job to rear the pheasants and arrange the shoots to which many of the Leek mill-owners came. They always had a big shoot on Boxing Day every year. Mum was born at Wardle Barn, and when she married Dad, they lived there for a couple of years and my older brother, Jim came along. Dad took over the job of water bailiff at Tittesworth reservoir (New Pool to the locals) in 1931. I was two years old when we moved to the bailiff's house below the dam. It was black and white timbered then, but while we were there, the top was taken down, rebuilt and pebbledashed.

Even though the reservoir was owned by Staffordshire Potteries Water Board, Mr Argles retained the shooting and fishing rights. He and Mr Watson each kept a boat there and they allowed anyone to fish for sixpence a day or one shilling per week, for which we issued the tickets. The money then had to be taken to Morton's jewellers, and then went to charity. Dad also had a rowing boat and he used to row to the top of the lake and cut sedges, which local farmers used to fetch to thatch their haystacks. I remember two people drowned themselves; one man left his cap on the bank and Dad had to go out in the boat with the police to drag for the bodies. We children were kept out of the way, but it still made a big impression on us.

Dad had to mow the embankments and keep everywhere tidy, and monitor the water levels and alter the sluice gates. The mills needed so much water out of the Churnet, so he had to regulate the flow.

The Churnet.

Until it was eventually piped down, he used to fetch all our drinking water from a spring. The rest of our water was got out of the 'Gauge Hole' which ran past the garden. And if he fancied a trout for supper, he caught one out of there. But I never liked trout. We only had paraffin lamps and the paraffin had to be carried from Leek, together with accumulators for the wireless, and of course all the groceries; although we grew a lot of vegetables, had an orchard and hens. Eventually we had a 'Jap' engine to supply electricity, which also ran a TV which my brother made with a six inch screen. What an achievement!

The Churnet was a favourite place for people to paddle in and picnic by, and used to be crowded at weekends and holidays. And we always had lots of visitors and relatives calling; it was such a lovely spot. Along with my two brothers we had an idyllic childhood. Our parents were wonderful; they never let us go anywhere, but friends were always down, and uncles came at weekends and we played cricket. Mr Grove, the vicar of Meerbrook was a regular visitor; he came shooting and fishing. When the overflow wasn't running, we'd sledge or rollerskate down it. My friend Nancy and I had one pair between us and we'd often just use one each. There was a green, slimy pool at the bottom which you had to avoid, but Nancy fell in it once; she was very smelly!

The Bailiff's House at the reservoir dam.

Dad used to take me to school at Ball Haye Green on the crossbar of his bike when he went to pick a paper up and go to Wardle Barn for milk. We went across the fields winding round by the Churnet. If we went round by the road, through Horsecroft to Tittesworth Avenue, there were nine gates to open and close. From school we went for our dinners to Gran at Wardle Barn, where I remember nearly every day we tied Aunty Mary to her chair with her apron strings.

We used to wear clogs at home and I was always with my Dad. One day he was chopping sticks and I put my foot on the block and said "Chop here!" as he was dropping the axe. The clog was split open but luckily my toes were intact and I was kept away after that. Dad used to cobble our shoes and clogs, he was very practical. We always went to Grandad's party at Wardle Barn on Christmas afternoon. We played games like postman's knock and skittles and sang round the piano. I remember going home once, it was dark and so foggy. Dad was carrying my younger brother Roy on his shoulders and we got lost going down the fields. When we got to Wardle Brook, Dad had to lie down to see which way the water was running, to know which way to go to find the bridge and the way home.

When the war started and the first siren went off, Dad pushed the table under the window and we got under it. I suppose we got braver and I remember standing at the front door at night watching German planes going over dropping lines of incendiary bombs down the valley. We went and picked some up the next morning and took them to the police station. I don't ever remember feeling frightened, we felt so protected by our parents.

In the evenings, ladies who didn't want to be seen walking up the main road to visit the Americans at Blackshaw Moor Army Camp would walk past, near to our home; there were quite a few of them. And later in the war there were a few Italian POWs from Blackshaw camp who would come down regularly and cut willows and sit on the embankment making baskets. Needless to say, I wasn't allowed to fraternise.

When I got married at Meerbrook Church, it was a very wet time. Wardle brook bridge had been washed away. Mr Prime couldn't get his taxis down the normal way through the gates, the road was so bad. So Maurice Brentnall managed to get his van down and loaded me, Mum and two bridesmaids up, all in wellies. Dad and my brother followed behind to push every time it got stuck. We changed into proper footwear at Prime's garage at Horsecroft. I don't remember how late we were, there were traffic lights on Blackshaw Moor and we went through them on red. I don't think it stopped raining all day.

When the reservoir was enlarged, the house was knocked down and buried under the new dam. Dad and Mum were moved into a water board house in Haregate Road and Dad continued working at the reservoir until he retired in 1968.

Jim Parker at Wardle Barn.

The Bailiff's house at Tittesworth Dam after it was refurbished

The Three Horseshoes, Blackshaw Moor, probably turn of the century.

Abraham Taylor was a gamekeeper for Sir Philip Brocklehurst and lived at Danebridge in one of Sir Philip's cottages.   He moved into the small Rockhall up on the Roches for two years in 1916. He'd had rheumatic fever, so he didn't pass for the army. In 1918, he moved to Newsett Farm, renting it from two ladies who lived at Bosley. He sold milk to Nestles at Congleton and because the roads around Meerbrook were then too bad for the milk lorries, he provided horses and wagon and picked up his neighbours milk from Brownsett, Roche Grange, Greenhouse and other road ends, and met the churn lorry at Crooked Chimney on the Macclesfield Road. In the summer when there was more milk, he ran two wagons and then Tom Skerratt helped to drive one. He kept seven horses and did the job from 1919 until 1931 when the roads were improved enough for the lorries to go round.

Mrs Taylor with cousins from London on the Queen's Seat at
the Roches.

Below: Abraham when they lived at Rock Hall.
Right: Rock Hall.

Above Abraham Taylor.

Left, Frank Taylor at Newsett.

Below left, Florrie Done and Freda Taylor on Cote Lane

Below, Mrs Taylor and London cousins in Ludchurch

Frank and Freda Taylor.

Abraham Taylor and his father Alfred.

Below: Mr Salt leaving Roche Grange about 1924.

Alec Day

In the 1930s, when Dad was farming Buttyfold, I remember him buying six or eight stirks from a sale at Bottomhouse, and in those days there were men who made their living droving cattle. That day Dad paid Tommy Malkin to walk those stock back to Buttyfold on his own, perhaps a distance of ten miles.

When I was at school, I remember walking a single barren cow to Leek Market. When you got to the Royal Oak at the bottom of Buxton Road, if you were lucky, there'd be two men waiting. One would be employed by Mottrams and the other by J. Oakes Ash, the two local auctioneers, who each had a separate ring to sell in, in the old market in Heywood Street. They would ask you which auctioneer would be selling your stock and then if that man was free, he'd help you to get your stock into the market.

This day, going up Ball Haye Street, the cow decided to bolt up a narrow alley to the back of the houses - there's a door on the alley now. You couldn't get past it to turn it back and it turned right towards Stockwell Street and into the doctor's garden. A maid came running out shouting "The baby! The baby!", terrified that the baby in a pram in the garden would get hurt. Luckily we got the cow out before any damage was done.

In 1937 or 38, the council were tar sealing the road from the chapel at Upperhulme, through the Dyeworks and up to Captain Brocklehurst's gate to Roches Hall. It was a stone road till then, so they put more stone on to level it and get a good surface and the water had to run off to the sides from the centre. Then they put tar and chippings on by hand. The tar was in 40 gallon barrels and had to be rolled up onto a tarpot and heated up. Then a man drew it off from a tap into a big watering can with a fan-shaped bar across the spout to spread the tar onto the road. While they were doing it, Dad asked if they would do the steep entrance into our yard. They put several loads of limestone down and tarred it. The estimated cost was £10 pounds and they came back for an extra shilling, so they were close to their price.

Nether Haye, below Buttyfold, was sold in the 1930s with 40 acres. Tatton's Mill bought it because the land bordered the Churnet. Dad rented the land from them. There were some of their dye pools on the land, three lots altogether, some on other land. The water from the dyehouse had to go through the pools to clear it before it went into the Churnet. In Nether Haye yard, there was a chamber into which they put blocks of alum for the contaminated water to flow over and help to purify it. There was a man employed to look after the pools and periodically a pool had to be closed off and the sediment cleared out.

The Yak from Capt Courtenay Brocklehurst's 'zoo'.

Brian Ball

The Hine family kept Dains Mill from 1802; four generations, all called Thomas. It was owned by the Harpur Crewe estate. Before that it was owned or run by Buttyfold Farm, which was then only about thirteen acres. My Great-grandad, Thomas was born in 1846 and died aged 91 in 1937. He was known as Billy Whiskers and when he retired and passed the business on to my Grandad Thomas, around about the end of the first war, he lived at Highgate Cottage, Rudyard. Most mornings, he'd walk from there to Stockmeadows Farm, Meerbrook, and then up to the mill, to arrive about 5 am to check if everyone was working

Grandad used to grind corn for local people and buy in corn to grind as well. The locally grown corn would probably be oats. I remember him telling me about a field to the right of Cat Tor, across the valley, joining the moor, which around the time of the first war won the prize for the best crop of oats in Staffordshire. They ground flour and oatmeal for human consumption and sold corn and bran.

There was a kiln house, three storeys high, which we've just restored. The top storey was for delivering the corn into. The middle storey was the drying floor. It had metal grating with ceramic tiles on top, two inches thick with tiny pin-holes all over. The bottom storey was the furnace hole. I would imagine the local grown grain would be dried there. Corn to be ground was fetched from Leek station with two horses and a wagon and when they got into Upperhulme a chain horse had to meet them and help drag it up the final bank. And if they had to go out

Dain's Mill showing the Kiln House.

the top way then, towards Moses Lane, they had to do the same. Later, steam wagons were used to fetch corn in, then Grandad bought the first petrol driven wagon in North Staffs. It was a 'Star' and Enoch Mountford used to drive it. One day they were delivering corn up to Captain Brocklehurst's menagerie, up at Roches Hall, and the old bull yak tipped the wagon over. They had to get it back onto its wheels and take it to be repaired.

I remember those yaks in the late forties. There was an old bull, a cow and a bull calf. The old ones died leaving the young bull. The estate brought some Highland cattle in to see if they would cross breed, but I don't think they did and they took them away.

Between the mill and the village, around 1925, Grandad set up a shop. Aunty Nelly and Mum ran it. They sold bread, flour and oatmeal, catering for locals and Tatton's Mill. I can remember going into Leek with Grandad to Tatton's Bakery in Heywood Street opposite the old cattle market, to fetch the bread. They just stacked the car up with loaves, on the floor, the back seats and the boot, full

Mr & Mrs William Hine and Mr & Mrs Edwin Pimlott
at Pheasant's Clough 1920s.

to the top. The shop was quite useful for the mill workers; they gave their order one day and picked up their groceries to take back on the bus the next day. Everything came in large sizes and was weighed out, sugar in blue bags, either one or two pounds -even down to pepper, weighed off in little packets. The shop closed after the war.

The mill closed around 1940 because Grandad was in hospital and there came a thunderstorm and because there was no-one to divert the water out of the pools the dam burst. It would have cost a lot to mend it and that type of milling was coming to an end, so they decided to close it. They kept poultry and pigs in it afterwards and stored hay on the lofts.

So in the shed which the shop was part of, Silcocks had a corn depot and Grandad managed it for them. The corn came from Leek station on three-wheeler Scammell

articulated trucks. They weren't very big, carrying 30 cwts or two tons. They were L.M.S. railway wagons. Then Mr Sims with his wagon delivered the corn out to farms. On Saturdays, when I was off school, he delivered to Swainsmoor so that I could go with him and open and close all the gates. There may have been nine I think.

Dain's Mill, probably 1930s.

Dain's Mill, probably 1930s.

Frank and Charles Belfield sheepwashing in the Churnet at Upperhulme in the late 1930s.

At Dain's Mill

Dain's Mill, Upperhulme, near Leek.

_____ 189 8

M^{rs}. M. Oliver. Executors. Wainsmoor

Bought of THOMAS HINE,
CORN ✶ DEALER ✶ AND ✶ MILLER.

TERMS—Cash, 5 per cent charged on all Accounts over due.

Feb	7	To L Horn 10/6 & cwt G Cake 9/6	1	0	0
	15	L Horn 11/- & 10st flour 14/-	1	7	0
		60 lbs Meal		7	0
	26	cwt G Cake		9	6
March 5		L Horn		11	0
	12	L Horn 11/- & 2 cwt G Cake 19/-	1	10	0
		Bag Bran 4/6 & Bag Combs 3/3		7	9
	24	L Horn 11/- & 60 lbs Med 7/6		18	6
April 7		L Horn 10/6 & L Horn 10/-	1	0	6
		2 cwt G Cake		19	0
	15	L Horn 10/6 & 4 Bags Combs 3/3	1	3	6
	28	L Horn 13/- & 2 cwts G Cake 19/-	1	12	0
		Bag Bran 4/9 & 2 Bags Combs 3/3		18	3
May 10		L Horn 13/- & L Horn 12/6	1	5	6
		10st flour 2/9 & 30 lbs Meal 4/-	1	4	0
	21	2 cwts G Cake 19/- & 2 Bags Bran 9/-	1	8	6
	23	L Horn		12	6
June 2		do		12	0
	9	½ L Galaty		6	0
	21	L Horn 10/- & Bag Bran 4/9		14	9
		10st flour 19/- & 30 lb Meal 4/- 1	3	9
		1 cwt 3 qrs 10 lbs Cotton Cake 9/-		13	0
July 1		2 cwts G Cake 19/- & Bag Bran 4/6	1	3	6
		2 cwts 5 lbs Cotton Cake 9/- & Bag Sharps 9/6 1	4	10
	7	L Horn 10/6 & L Horn 10/-	1	0	6
Augt 4		L Horn 10/6 & L Horn 10/-	1	0	6
		10st flour 15/6 & Bag Bran 4/3		19	9

Mr Hine and family at Dain's Mill, and another view of his Bull-nose Morris at Meerbrook.

Grandad was very proud of his car and often gave people a lift to church - unless sometimes when it was raining he might not because they would get the upholstery wet.

The Hine girls, Nora, Fanny, Maggie, Cissie and Nellie.

A group of village men and boys who had worked on new paths for the church, c 1930s.

1. Vic Moss	2. Frank Robinson	3. Arnold Moss	4. Arthur Coates
5. Joe Heath	6. Jack Robinson	7. Enza Barks	8. Joe Mellor
9. Jabez Mellor	10. Sid Barks	11. Bill Mellor	12. Tom Robinson
13. Jack Clulow	14. Joe Robinson	15. Eric Moss	16. Arthur Barlow
17. Les Holland	18. Bill Allen	19. Stephen Hine	20. Henry Beardmore
21. Bill Hine	22. Joe Hine	23. Mr Grove	24. Tom Hine
25. John Moss	26. Ken Ryder		

Freda Fernyhough

When I was a young child we lived at Red Shaw Farm. A number of the local farmers worked over the road in the Gun stone pits. They'd have a small farm and their wives and children helped to keep that going while they were at work. During the depression, this work would make the difference between success and failure. What sticks in my mind about that time, Mum told me that one local family were able to swap their hessian sack hearth rug for a proper one.

One pit was the council pit and Mr Mellor and my father, Mr Warrington, worked that pit. The stone was good for road mending, the men broke it and filled wooden containers of one cubic yard, which would weigh a ton. They were paid piecework on that. The other pits were owned by Sneyd Colliery, as was Red Shaw Farm. They liked the stone for making hard blue engineering bricks. They built a hut for some of the men who came from the Potteries to live in during the week, and so save transport. But these men couldn't abide the countryside and refused to stay. I think they must have missed the pubs and social life at night. They thought it was terrible stuck up on the side of Gun Hill.

But to me, what was so sad was that mother's brother George came home from the Trenches only to be killed by a truck that came off the rails in the stone pits. A bitter blow.

At Gun stone pits.   Jack Knight and Joe Mellor.

Both of these photos show New Grange Farm when Robinsons were there, the top one about 1960 just before its demolition and the construction of the new reservoir. There were actually two New Grange farms next door to each other - see also the photo on page 60.

The Robinson family at
New Grange.

Mr Robinson and Tom at
New Grange.

Below; The Abbey Farm
drawn by Mackaness 1890.

Milk churns at New Grange.

Right: Frank Robinson and his father
at New Grange.

Below: Tom Robinson.

The Robinson children on the footbridge over the ford on the way to New Grange.
It is now under the reservoir.

INVOICE   Telephone: LEEK 557

L. HOLLAND 998

AGRICULTURAL AND MOTOR ENGINEER
Spraying   Welding   Panel Beating   Battery Charging

NEW GRANGE GARAGE, MEERBROOK, Nr. LEEK

M͞ J Belfield

July   19͞3͞2

July	1	8 Gals Petrol	1	14	6
		Repair Unit Handle		2	0
	3	Journey to remove Casting on Swap.			
		Weld same, Journey to refit		19	6
	6	7 Gals Petrol	1	10	2½
	10	2 Gals Petrol		8	7½
	13	7 Gals Petrol	1	10	2½
	16	10 Gals Petrol	2	2	9
		Charge Wireless Battery			6
		2 Journeys to Tractor		9	0
		Vulcanise Cover Both sides		12	0
		Vulcanise Tube, refit Tyre		6	6
	20	7 Gals Petrol	1	10	2½

Local farmers watch as another bale of wool is weighed by Mr C. Bagshaw of Earl Sterndale at Leek's Annual Wool Sale in the Butter Market, around 1960. Looking on: Mr W. Hall (Waterfall), Mr F. Allen (Grindon), Mr J. Bennison (Tittesworth), Mr T. Robinson (Meerbrook), Mr C. Heath (Longsdon), Mr J. Barks (Blackshaw Moor), Mr F. Belfield (Meerbrook) and Mr G. Austin (Grindon).

WI trip, Mrs Whitehouse, Mrs Burgess, Mrs Barks, Mrs Heath, ?1930s.

Mr Nadin, Bent Farm, Gun End.

The Primrose League. Whist Drive and Dance held at Meerbrook Village Hall winter 1931/32. The proceeds went to subscriptions to gain 'recommends' for hospital treatment. About £90 was raised and Alice Hine won the main prize which was a tea service.

Back row: Alice Hine (Mrs George Barks), Elsie Hine (Mrs Frank Taylor), Jessie Clulow (Mrs Tom Hine), Mrs Harriet Barks (Blackshaw Moor), Mrs Worth (Nether Hay), Hilda Mellor (Mrs Cyril Hine), Vinnie Barks (Mrs Jack Clulow), John Clulow (Jack)

Middle row: Madge Mellor (The Lea), Sidney Brown (Pheasant's Clough, son of William), Charlie Belfield (Hurdlow), William Barks (Blackshaw Moor), William Mellor (Green Lane Farm), Mary Bennison (Tittesworth Farm, Mrs Alec Brown), Alec Brown (Pheasant's Clough), Mrs Hine (Roche Side, mother of Alice, back row)

Front row: Mary Robinson (Mary Findlow, Buxton Brow), John Clulow Snr and Alice Clulow (Broad Lea), William Brown Snr (Pheasant's Clough), Mrs William Mellor (Green Lane), Tom Cooper (Frith Bottom Farm), George Mellor (Son of Madge Mellor, The Lea).

Compiled by Gerald Robinson

The Village Hall.

THE MEERBROOK VILLAGE HALL

The Village Hall was known as the Public Room from 1908-1929. It was the brain child of a group of local people who enjoyed dancing but were not allowed to do so after midnight in the Schoolroom.

Entertainment around the turn of the century was the occasional dance or whist drive & dance - and some of these were in aid of Primrose League funds. The Whist would be between 8.00 and 10.30pm fullowed by dancing until 2am and sometimes even longer.

Money for the Building Fund was raised by shares and subscriptions and the work was carried out by Mr. T.H. Mellor of Green Lane Farm, the local joiner and wheelwright.

The land was leased for 21 years from Mr. John Clulow of Broad Lea Farm, at an annual rent of £1. The building, which was of tongue and groove boarding with a corrugated iron roof, was about 45 feet by 16 feet, with a small room at one end to serve as a cloakroom.

The Room was opened in May 1908 by Mrs. Anthony Ward of Leek and was known locally as the Bungalow. The cloakroom was enlarged by one yard in 1915 so that refreshments could be provided. Toilet facilities were very primitive, only an outside loo. Lighting was by hanging oil-lamps, heating was negligible. Valor oil stoves were carried from homes when the Room was used. Water was provided in churns and heated for tea-making and washing up on double-burner oil-stoves.

It is worth noting that apart from the usual local fund raising, money was raised for the Soldiers and Sailors Association during the First World War and in 1915 a dance was held and the proceeds of £3-5-0d given to the Red Cross Hospital in Leek to buy a bed to be known as the Meerbrook Bed.

In 1919 the school managers joined the Public Room Committee to further the use of the Room and money was raised to give presents to the Meerbrook and Upperhulme soldiers returning from the War, and also towards the Memorial in Church. A Young Man's Club was formed in 1920 and meetings were held in the room.

When the lease expired in 1929 the shareholders wished to sell the Room, which was bought by Mr. Edward Hulton, the prospective Conservative candidate for Leek, who handed it over to the Leek Branch of the Primrose League.

The Primrose League owned the Hall between 1929-1953. It was an organisation founded in 1883 in memory of Benjamin Disraeli. Mrs. C. Lomas of Roach Grange was the Warden for Meerbrook area. When she left the district in 1927 her place was taken by Mrs Taylor of New Sett, with the help of sub-wardens Mr W. Brown, Mrs J. Clulow and Mrs Ager, who were joined by Miss P. Ager, Miss J. Clulow, Miss W. Taylor, Mr. S. Brown and Mr. J. Clulow (Jnr.), and later Mrs Joyce Robinson, as a committee to run the Room and raise money for the Primrose League.

The sub-wardens collected the yearly subscriptions of sixpence each, and each member had a yellow badge in the shape of a Primrose - a stud for the gent's lapel - a brooch for the ladies.

A special Whist Drive and Dance was arranged every year for Primrose League funds. In 1939 it was decided to enlarge the width of the Room by six feet and add another cloakroom, the work being carried out by Mr. J. Findlow, the local builder and joiner. Electricity was installed as a supply had recently been brought to the village, and together these improvements cost £74-6-1d.

After war broke out in September 1939 all homes and buildings had to be blacked out during times of lighting - even car head lamps had to be hooded. All events in the Room had to finish at 10pm. The Room was registered as an Emergency venue and 24 mattresses were stored in a bedroom at New Grange Farm - fortunately they were never needed.

The Home Guard used the Room regularly and in 1943 provided the money for new blackout curtains. On two occasions soldiers were billeted in the Room for short periods, scrubbing the floor before they left! Lots of polish and elbow grease had to be used by volunteers before the next dance.

W.V.S duties were undertaken by Mrs G.M. Nicholson. President of the Womens Institute.

Meerbrook Fete and Sports day in the early 1950s.

Special Drives for National Savings were held throughout the country and Mrs Nicholson and her helpers would be in the Room to take the money and supply the Savings Certificates. On each occasion Meerbrook would reach the target set for the village and were awarded special certificates.

A band of ladies knitted hundred-weights of navy. airforce and khaki wool, in balaclavas, socks and gloves for the forces, and they were responsible for raising money to send gifts to all the local men and women in the forces at Christmas time.

Sugar was allowed to Womens' Institutes for jam making from surplus fruits from local gardens and blackberry picking. Members carried double-burner oil-stoves, jam kettles, fruit and jam jars to the Room and then the jars were taken to New Grange Farm to be covered and labelled by Mrs W. Hine and Mrs Nicholson. They were stored until passed by a government examiner, after which they could be sold to a shopkeeper as part of his rationed allowance. A canning machine was also obtained and surplus fruit such as peaches and apples were preserved in this way for the local people.

After the V.E. celebrations in 1947 a committee was formed, with Mrs Nicholson, Chairman, Mrs W. Hine, Secretary, and Mr E. Barks, Treasurer, to start a Building Fund. A Sports Day was organised every year along with indoor events.

By 1950 the Primrose League had declined and in 1953 the Leek Branch was disbanded and a decision taken to dispose of the Room at Meerbrook. An open meeting was convened of a Building Fund Committee and it was agreed to buy the Room for the village and to abandon the idea of building a new village hall. The Primrose League Committee was willing to sell for £50 and Mrs G.M. Nicholson and the committee proceeded, then immediately turned it over to the village for the use of the people of Meerbrook. It was to be known from then on as the Meerbrook Village Hall. Four trustees were appointed: Mr T. Hine, Mr J. Clulow, Mr J. Mountfort and Mrs W. Hine.

The members of the Fund Raising Committee together with the Trustees formed the new management committee and £400 already raised was handed over to Village Hall Funds. Mrs Nicholson donated a Grand Piano and her mother, Mrs Evans gave twenty-four canvas seated chairs - much appreciated as the only other seats were wooden forms around the Room.

When the Potteries Water Board bought up most of the properties in Meerbrook, the land on which the hall stood was included, but a twenty-one year lease was granted.

The Hall could be hired for five shillings per hour and was being used, apart from meetings, for whist drives and dances, by a flourishing Youth Club and by the local school children for P.T. lessons.

Water still had to be carried in chums until 1975 when the Severn Trent (as the Potteries Water Board had then become) brought water into the Village and the old Village Pump became redundant. Water laid on brought more improvements to the kitchen and the long awaited new toilets were installed at a cost of £2,800 with a grant of £1,500 towards the cost by the Staffs County Council.

In 1983 The Village Hall was able to buy the ground from Severn Trent for £10, Mr J. Clulow withdrawing his legal rights to buy this land which he previously owned.

The Village Hall now wholly belongs to Meerbrook. In July 1988 work was commenced to extend and encase the building in stone. The main contractors were local lads Raymond and Leslie Hine. Many committee members volunteered their labour and particularly Mr Jack Robinson, Norman Goodwin, Bernard Machin, Clifford Moss, Donald Robinson, Graham Robinson, Reg Robinson, Keith Simcock and Geoff Woodward. The total cost was over £21,000

A Ladies team included Hilda Allen, Elsie Barks, Ivy Goodwin, Louie Machin, Margaret Moss Marilyn Willshaw and Joan Woolliscroft, who cleaned and painted the Hall.

An official opening was held on Saturday November 12th 1988 when Mr Eric Moss, one of the oldest local residents, performed the opening ceremony in front of a large audience.

With acknowledgements to W. Hine, M. Heath and J. Clulow, from their Village Hall booklet, 1996.

The ladies of Meerbrook, always famous for their hospitality.

Mrs Margaret Robinson, Mrs Fanny Pimlott, Mrs Gladys Hine, Mrs Vinnie Clulow and Mrs Alice Riley.

Pantomine at the Village Hall 1960s.

Meerbrook
schoolchildren at
the seaside trips
in the 1950s.

At Meerbrook School Sports in the late 1950s.

Rev and Mrs Walmsley, Meerbrook Fete 1984

At the Three Horseshoes in Meerbrook.

Meerbrook School early 1950s.